Love and Licks for Woofs to the Wise

"Disarming and clever, witty and thoughtful, charming and life-affirming, *Woofs to the Wise* is a book of manners like no other. It will give you food for thought and tug at your heart strings as it reminds you that civility and good manners are not trivial, because they do the everyday busy work of goodness."

— P. M. Forni
Professor, Johns Hopkins University
author of *Choosing Civility:*
The Twenty-Five Rules of Considerate Conduct

"When you feel like life has you licked, read this book."
— Neil Izenberg, M.D.
CEO, KidsHealth.org

"By the time you've read this heartfelt correspondence an amazing thing will have happened: you've learned how to get along in this world. With humans and dogs alike."
— Jerry and Eileen Spinelli
Prize-winning children's book authors

"*Woofs to the Wise* offers powerful lessons not only in civility but in friendship and life."

— Lyudmila Bloch
Founder of www.EtiquetteOutreach.com

"I follow the advice of wise and witty women in my life; it's smart and fun. I also follow dogs; it's smart and fun too. And here we have both, together. What's not to like about that?"

— Kevin Walsh
Author of *Follow the Dog Home*

"*Woofs to the Wise* is enlightening, touching and funny. Two enthusiastic paws up! The correspondence between ZsaZsa and Nessa delightfully reminds us of what's important in life and how to be the best we can be. Thanks to ZsaZsa's new found fame, my two dogs are now requesting their own email accounts and are planning to write their first novel."

— Cyndi Edwards
TV Host "Daytime"

"No one really lives until they share their life with a canine companion. The witty words from the heart from divas ZsaZsa and Nessa will enlighten you to the most significant lessons in life. An engaging dialogue! A must-read and must-share book!!"

— Dixie Eng
General Manager, Olde Towne Pet Resort, Springfield, VA

Woofs to the Wise

Learning to Lick at Life and Chew On Civility

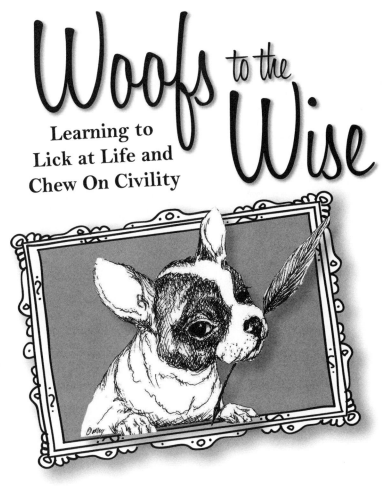

Mary M. Mitchell & Nessa Forman

Illustrated by Oatley Kidder

TMO Press
Seattle, WA

FOREWORD BY LETITIA BALDRIGE

Hardcover ISBN13: 978-0-9852532-1-9

Library of Congress Control Number: 2012937228

Printed in the USA

10   9   8   7   6   5   4   3   2   1

Woofs to the Wise:

When you believe in something,
go ahead and write about it!

Contents

A Dog's Life

Top Dogs & New Tricks

Work Like a Dog

Get Along, Little Doggie

The Tail End

Special Treats

The Chief Characters:
Around ZsaZsa, clockwise
from lower left:
Mary, Jim, Peloton, and Nessa.

The Illustrator:
Oatley Kidder

Zsa Zsa

List of Illustrated
Woofs to the Wise

Zsa Zsa

Foreword

Although I have had the pleasure of being guardian to a long line of Jack Russell terriers, highly regarded for their cleverness, I have never had a dog nearly so articulate as ZsaZsa, who rises to the top like cream, because she is simply the best. She even has it over the many dogs that have inhabited the White House in the last fifty years, all of whom have had a good sniff of me, and vice versa.

I pride myself on knowing a good deal about civility, yet I must say that I have learned a lot from ZsaZsa in reading this book. I intend to communicate regularly with her from now on. Furthermore, I am considering asking her to collaborate with me on my next book, which may focus on the differences in temperament, which are considerable, between First Dogs of Democrat Administrations and their Republican counterparts.

Letitia Baldrige
Washington, D.C.

[Ms. Baldrige appeared on the cover of *Time* magazine, where she was hailed as "America's leading arbiter of manners." Author of twenty-seven books, she served as Social Secretary to the Kennedy White House.]

Prologue

Frankly, this book came about because I failed to keep my research assistant busy enough. Not one to sit idly by, Wayne set up an email account for our dog. At first my husband, Jim, and I thought this was a cute—if somewhat frivolous—idea.

That was before Nessa, a long-time friend of mine, more accurately my sister-of-choice, started driving me nuts with questions about what we would be doing on the Saturday when she (finally!) came out from Philly to visit us in Seattle. Problem was that Saturday was six weeks away. I hadn't even set my schedule for that day yet.

Now ZsaZsa, our French bulldog, is a very clear communicator. She lets us know when she is happy, sad, miffed, hungry, tired, ready to play, and many more things. All right, so she can't type. But through her, I was able to say things to Nessa that I would not have had the nerve to say directly. Like, "Come on, Nessa. Give me a break here. Get real. We've got lots of time yet."

Thing is, we don't always have as much time as we think, or would like to have.

ZsaZsa, in coming right out and telling it like it was, really ingratiated herself with Nessa. She, in turn, quickly picked up on the fact that there are things that you can only tell your dog. This type of special communication is possible even if it isn't your own dog, so long as you come to a certain understanding. ZsaZsa and Nessa came to understand one another very well, very quickly.

ZsaZsa, when awake, can be quite curious. She clearly wants to improve her lot in life. She perceives that she is not so much like other dogs. Nessa soon came to appreciate this fact.

So a rather lengthy and somewhat quirky correspondence developed, which Jim and I were only too glad to facilitate. And Nessa did finally come out to Seattle, where ZsaZsa taught her the meaning of patience and how to live in the moment, as well as where to cadge the best treats.

Of course, the conversation thread didn't stop when Nessa returned to Philadelphia. One thing led to another—not the least of which were Nessa's suggestions for ZsaZsa's career. Hence this book, which was Nessa's idea, obviously with the approval of ZsaZsa.

Nessa looked at it this way:

"When I received my first email from ZsaZsa, I welcomed the correspondence, and the amusing distraction of a canine telling me about her life on a houseboat in Seattle. She called me Auntie Ness and asked a lot of questions. I advised her as best I could (she can be very bull-headed … it's in the genes). I asked her many questions as well. Even though we were very different—separated by a continent, our ages, our species, and our outlooks on life (I have never been one to be patient, or in the moment) — ZsaZsa's brilliance as a therapeutic dog won me over. So did her crying need for a new career, since Jim had closed his surgical practice and she could no longer be a therapy dog. Clearly, here was a dog who would not be content to loll around and live life from one treat to the next. Plus, I perceived some real Diva potential here. And a real Diva is not to be underestimated.

"As I read over our email exchanges, I found them to be instructive, amusing, irreverent, and witty. The emails made important points about relationships and communication. They also reminded me of a book Mary, my sister-of-choice, had given me long ago, when she was in charge of public relations for the Walnut Street Theatre and I was arts editor for *The Philadelphia Bulletin*. The book was *84 Charing Cross Road*, and it was a story that unfolded through a series of letters. So ZsaZsa, Mary, and I agreed to share our story through emails and began work as quickly as possible. We wrote in the moment because there wasn't a millisecond to waste."

Little did we know at the time how true that was …

Mary M. Mitchell

This is really my book, and here is how I see it:

My full name is ZsaZsa LaPooch. I am cute, adorable, and five years old. I love being scratched in all the right places. You may give me treats any time.

I have lots to say, and I am a very clear communicator. Since I don't have a tail to wag around (I was born that way, if you must know), I have to use my eyes and my nice, big ears, as well as a variety of snorfles, growls, barks, whines, grunts, and howls to make my point; except of course when Mary or Jim are helping me put my thoughts into words, because I have trouble using a keyboard. Left to my own desserts (yum), I often stop to leap from a lap to the floor to scare away potential intruders. My guardians do their best to keep me on track.

I really loved corresponding with my Auntie Ness, who lived far away in Philadelphia. She came out to visit me so I could teach her how to scratch me just right. I also taught her a lot of other things, as you will see.

Now, in fairness, Auntie Ness taught me some things too. As well she should have, since she was on this planet a lot longer than I will ever be. She taught me to lick at life and chew on civility. She was a Diva and my sounding board as I figured out what I wanted to do with my life. I had a lot of career ideas. She helped me find the best one for me.

Auntie Ness was my mentor. And I was her "niecette-of-choice." Good Dog, how I miss her.

My godmother Oatley has painted my portrait in two places on the walls of our floating home in Seattle. She scoped out our other place, an apartment where Mary and I each have offices (My office is a special place under the bed that only I can squeeze into.), but she hasn't put any painting of me on the walls there (yet). She did make a drawing of me as a young author. She's very talented, and her drawings are a big part of this book, scattered around like so many tasty treats.

Mary, Jim, and Auntie Ness have helped me bunch my correspondence into five main categories: A Dog's Life; Top Dogs and New Tricks; Work Like a Dog; Get Along, Little Doggie; and The Tail End. I wanted one more section on How to Bring up Guardians—a thought I've been chewing on for quite some time. But they outvoted me, even though this is *my book*. That's okay, though. I will get my licks in anyway.

In Special Treats, I give you a sampling of the way I choose to interpret my guardians' "commands" if you must call them that. I prefer to call them Approved List of Suggestions for Collaborative Communication. When you get to know me better, you will understand why. I think you might also want to have a look at My Very Own Diary and my first-ever blog called "ZZsTreat."

If you, Dear Reader, have some suggestions for my next book or my blog, please email me. I have my own email account: zzlapooch@gmail.com. I usually respond within a few days.

Even better, if you come to Seattle, and you bring treats, I'll let you see me in the flesh. But first, have your people call my people. Some days I am pretty busy. Most days I am just pretty.

ZsaZsa LaPooch

Woofs to the Wise:

Enjoy what's going on right now.
Don't worry about yesterday.

A Dog's Life

Hello & Woof

Dear Ms. Forman,

I am ZsaZsa LaPooch. Surely you know who I am. I hear a lot about you from my guardians, Mary and Jim.

I am writing because I learned that you are coming to Seattle to visit us at our floating home. I also know that you and Mary have been friends forever and ever and ever, but, even so, Mary says that some of the questions you ask her are really irritating.

As I'm sure Mary has told you, I am not just any dog. I am a real original. I am five years old and very cute— I know because everyone says so. And I make people feel good. Dr. Jim, you probably know, is a real MD. Fancy that! Before he stopped seeing patients, he used to bring me to his office. My job was to calm people down and make them feel good. I always welcomed patients at the door, and I managed to get lots of treats. They did too—their treats were me.

So I have decided to make it my job to help you. I understand that you want details about your upcoming visit to Seattle from Philadelphia, and that you want them six weeks in advance.

You may not know this, but Mary can't focus on what time the Seattle Art Museum is open tomorrow, let alone six weeks from now. I know this because she keeps muttering that she is just trying to get through today. I also understand from her that you can be quite the Diva when you want to be. So, to facilitate matters, I am asking you to be my pawpal. I wouldn't mind learning something about being a Diva.

Sincerely,

Miss LaPooch

Dear Ms. LaPooch:

Of course I know who you are. But how did you get my email address? For that matter, how is it you have your own email address? I hope you haven't hacked into my computer or credit card accounts. Should I be wary? Should I call the police or juvenile authorities?

You sound very presumptuous, like many of the young women I have mentored over the years. So many of them were in great need of guidance. But I am not sure I can take on your case. It is questionable—and maybe even criminal—to email me without a proper introduction from Mary. I should think you would know that, since Mary is such an expert on the subject of manners and etiquette.

What is all this business about treats anyway? Why are you so motivated by rewards from other people? The best reward is to know you have done a good job and met your goals.

For your information, Mary has been my friend for a very long time. I frequently went to her family home for holidays when she lived in Philadelphia, and we have remained close, even though we now live far apart. I miss seeing Mary as often as I used to, but it's a good thing she moved to Seattle. Good for Jim; good for you.

Now, since I certainly do know Mary, I will consider a relationship with you, although this seems highly irregular. I mean, really—emails with a dog? Now that I am retired, I am looking for a project, a "third act" if you will. You could be at the top of my list, because I see from your email that you need instruction.

So, Ms. LaPooch, you may email back, but please be respectful. We are, after all, of two different generations. We have a lot to teach each other, but only if we hear what each has to say with an open mind and an open heart ... listen to understand, not just respond. I should know something about this because I was a communications executive for many years at WHYY in Philadelphia. We'll discuss Philadelphia more later.

Sincerely,

Nessa Forman

Woofs to the Wise:

Listen to understand,
not just respond.

Dear Ms. Forman,

I am so excited that you will be my pawpal. I have no idea why you think I need instruction, but I am a young dog who loves to learn new tricks, so I will humor you. Besides, I have so much to tell you about my life and how I keep everyone in line ... humans and canines.

My boyfriend Peloton is a black Puggle with a white chest and paws that make him look like he is in formal attire with spats. However, there is nothing formal in the goofy way he acts. I will undoubtedly have more to tell you about him later.

I only have one best girlfriend, named Bailey. She is an older Pomeranian and is a neighbor dog here on the dock, near our floating home in Seattle. I hate to admit it, but she is kind of the boss of me, mostly because she got here first. I know that you and Mary are best girlfriends. Is one of you the boss of the other? How did you meet?

Now that we are officially pawpals, what should I call you? You may call me ZsaZsa. Sometimes people call me ZZ. I respond to either of these, provided there is a treat. Will you send me treats? Will you bring treats from Philadelphia? I have heard a little bit about Philadelphia, but I want to hear more about pretzels and cheese-steaks. Scratch that—just bring me some. Make sure they are fresh, not stale. I will make up my own mind. I am a French bulldog who happens to like treats of all kinds, and guests are supposed to bring gifts.

I like to eat at Norm's, which is the only dog-friendly restaurant here in Seattle. Steve, the owner, gives me treats because I am so adorable. I also like to go there with Mary and Jim for a snort during Happy Hour. When I sit at Mary's feet under the table, people walk by and tell me I am a chick magnet. I have learned to accept this. I like all the pats I get when I am there.

You asked why I have an email account. Why shouldn't I have one? Do you discriminate against dogs?

Do you like snorfles? Please answer me right away.

Your new and best friend,

ZZ

Dear ZZ:

Okay, Okay. So you have an email account. So be it.

Mary is much more than a "girlfriend," and I am too much of a Diva to refer to our relationship in such a manner. Mary is my sister-of-choice. We first met when I was a writer and editor—and a kick-ass one at that—at a newspaper called *The Philadelphia Bulletin* (of blessed and sainted memory). Do you even know what a newspaper is? So many young people don't appreciate them anymore.

My job at the *Bulletin* was to put high and low culture on the first page (You would have the advantage over me at appreciating low culture.) and show how art can affect the daily lives of ordinary people (and, I suppose, dogs). Mary worked for the Walnut Street Theater, where her job was to pester me into giving the theater a daily headline.

Truth be told, I believe Mary was a little bit afraid of me back then. I think a lot of people were. More than a few people called me a "tough old broad" (and worse) behind my back, and even sometimes to my face! Although I didn't mind (much), I preferred to think of myself as a Diva. Mary did her job, and did it well, which is a quality I always respect.

When my beloved *Bulletin* closed, and I was going through a difficult time, Mary could see that I was hurting. She reached out to me and, in so doing, taught me the most important lesson of all: what true friendship means. We never thought about being bossy. We did help each other see things differently when we just were so upset that we could not think straight.

So, yes, you may call me Auntie Ness. I can't wait to meet you when I visit Seattle. But I will say this to you: It is not nice to ask for a present from someone you haven't even met. You are being naughty. Try to behave. You will be richly rewarded. I am sure that Mary tells you a lot about good behavior.

Not sure about Jim. I hear he can be pretty wild and crazy.

You are right that a guest should bring treats for her hostess. But remember too, please, that people who are visiting sometimes worry that they are imposing on their hosts. The biggest treat you can give any person is to make them feel like they are at home when they are around you. After all, a host's primary concern is to see that guests enjoy themselves.

Will you meet me at the airport? Will you provide a limo? If so, I hope there will be treats in the limo, as well as a glass of bubbly (my favorite "snortful"—that, by the way, is the correct way to spell the word). Will there be a mani-pedi person, as well as a masseuse and a hair stylist in the limo? After all, I am a 21st century Diva. From what I see of your nature, you are an extremely fresh dog. Beware! Your Auntie Ness is on to you!

Love and Licks,

Auntie Ness

Dear Auntie Ness,

Thank you for being my Aunt! And for writing back so soon.

I can tell that we are going to have lots to say to each other. This is my first time as a host, and I want to get it all right. Everyone feels at home around me. I always let people know how happy I am to see them. Unlike all the other dogs I know, I cannot wag what little tail I have. (Please do not kid me about this; it is a sore subject with me.)

I move my beautiful big ears around and bring over one of my many tennis balls, inviting people to play with me, or at least to give me a few scratches. This always makes our guests smile and feel especially welcome. You'll see. I'll show you how it is done.

Be sure to let us know what time you arrive, so we can meet you at the airport. Whether you are a guest or a host, you are always performing for each other, except when you are sleeping. So naturally we'll plan lots of naps. I am very big on naps. I never seem to get enough of them.

Of course I know what a newspaper is. I used them often when I was a puppy. Now, I just go outside when I need to do my business.

Gotta run. Peloton is out in the hall waiting for me.

ZsaZsa

2

Boyfriends

Dear Auntie Ness,

Now that we are pawpals, I think we may have a pedigree in common. Perhaps some ancestor of yours was a littermate with one of mine? You see, I know that I don't look too much like Mary or Jim. They are much bigger, although when I wriggle myself into position in their bed, I take up just as much room (or more) than they do.

I think I already mentioned to you that I have a boyfriend. His name is Peloton. He lives right down the hall from the apartment where Mary and I have our separate offices. We have been best friends for most of my life. He is a little older—but not any wiser—than I. He is definitely not as clever as I am either, which comes in handy when we play. Usually, I get my nips in, but big people walk by very hesitantly, because they think we are mad at each other. We go about snarling, biting, and chasing each other up and down the corridors.

Peloton is always hungry, and he tries to push his way into our place every time his guardians walk by our door. When he does get in, he heads right for my food bowl. He shakes and wiggles his entire body to keep me away. Then he wolfs down all of *my* food! He doesn't savor a single gulp, and even looks all over for *more* to eat. He doesn't ever acknowledge me until he gets chased into the hallway again.

That's when I get up on my hind legs (which I am very good at), and I beguile him into playing with me. Mary says it is self-defense, but I think it is love. I can feint one way, do a rolling cross-body block on him the other way, and knock his pins out from under him. When our guardians tell us it is quitting time, he almost always gives me a little kiss, and I sometimes paw him on his shoulder.

I often go to the dog park with a bunch of other dogs. You won't be surprised to hear that I am boss of all of them. I might be the smallest dog in the group, but I am also the smartest. When we go for runs, if I get tired, I let them run their foolish paws off. Then I am all rested and ready to go when they come back. Maybe when you come for your visit, you can see for yourself. Unlike Mary, I am able to plan ahead.

Love and licks,

ZsaZsa

Dear ZsaZsa:

It is possible that we may share a pedigree. After all, I believe we all have a little mutt in our background—and a black sheep or two. Are we related? Possibly. Should we do a DNA test? I think not. I think we can be an Auntie and niece-by-choice. These are the best kinds of "family" to have. You know that Mary and I are sisters-of-choice. That is a good thing, as you will see now that you are my niecette-of-choice.

This brings us to Peloton. By the way, what kind of name is that? Does he look like a Greek God, or even a Viking?

Peloton appears to be your boyfriend-of-choice. In Philadelphia, where I come from, we do not usually bite boyfriends. (Though, we might smack them around from time to time, whether they need it or not.) By the way, ZZ, are you even old enough to have a boyfriend? Does Mary know that you and this Peloton are playing "Spin the Dog Bone"?

You must tell me more about this misguided Peloton. It sounds like we may have to whip that pooch into shape to make him serious boyfriend material. He sounds like he is misbehaving on purpose, to get your attention. Well …*mon Dieu!* (That is French, of course, for "My Dog," but then you would know that, wouldn't you?)

However, since you are the alpha pooch, you must use your powers for the good. Even though no one is the boss of you, you are the boss of all. Use that power well, my dear ZsaZsaLa. We don't want Peloton to start hanging out with other down-in-the-mouth pooches that don't bite. Still, I think, if this is the way you and Peloton want to behave, and you both bite each other equally, without drawing blood, it's probably okay—if it works for you.

Let me give you a real lesson in love. Your boyfriend is the one for you if he makes you feel super special about yourself, if he makes you feel smarter, sexier, and like the most beautiful pooch on the planet. It is all about whether he brings out the best in you. In your case, a little bite and nip is a love tap. Because it is about *you* and how your heart goes pitter-patter when Peloton enters your realm.

But I must ask you: does Peloton also allow you to eat his food? He should. Maybe you can teach him that it's not a good thing to eat from someone else's plate, unless you return the favor.

As for the dog park, Zeeez, that is a treat I don't want to miss, so long as it isn't rainy and muddy while I am in Seattle. Since we are getting to know each other better, I will educate you about the role and joy of being a highly evolved Diva. This—and cuteness—are extremely significant topics and should not be left to chance. And this is more important than finding your next treat.

Real Divas tend to be mature, worldly-wise women. Because of their life experience and smarts, Divas have a responsibility to teach and mentor the next generation. Mary and I have been honored to have had excellent

Diva teachers and mentors. Let me quote a former Secretary of State, Madeleine Albright: "There is a special place in hell (excuse my French) for women who do not help other women."

By the way, ZZZZZZZZZZZZZZZs, guys don't have the heart and soul to be Divas. They are all about solving problems. But we, the fairer and smarter sex, are about building relationships. Take this to heart.

We'll communicate again soon. I am sure of it.

Until then,

Your Auntie Ness

Dear Auntie Ness,

I have so many things to tell you, and so many questions. I don't know anything about Philadelphia, but I think anyone from there must be very smart. I heard Jim and Mary talk about a Dr. Ben Franklin, and he sounded awfully smart. Did he invent rice? I don't care much for rice, unless there is a lot of meat juice on it.

You asked before if I ever ate Peloton's food. Well, that I do not do. That's because he never has food out at his place; I don't think food stays in his bowl for more than a few seconds.

I just eat when I am hungry. Mary and Jim leave food in my bowl all the time. My favorite time to eat is late at night. (I am French, after all.) I prefer privacy while I dine, although I know they don't mind if I participate in their mealtimes. I sit there, looking cute and generally indispensable. As long as I don't whine, they give me a little nibble here and there, just like the people in banks, at UPS, and the bakery. When you come out to visit, just stick with me. I know where to go to get all kinds of treats.

One nice thing about Peloton is that he doesn't try to gobble my treats, as long as we both get one. I tend to savor mine, just to show him who is the boss. I guess our gentle breeding shows in the way we share.

I have been to all of Peloton's birthday parties, and he always comes to mine. Usually we go to Norm's restaurant. It is my favorite because it is the only one where I am welcome inside. I will tell you more about Norm's some time, or, better yet, I'll take you there! What do you say?

Licks and snorfles
(which is absolutely the correct way to spell it!),

ZZ

Dear ZZ:

You are talking about two different Bens here: Dr. Benjamin Franklin is a Founding Father and famous Philadelphian. Uncle Ben's is a brand of rice. I will have to get you a history book about famous Bens and the *Dogs Who Helped Change Our Lives and Altered World History.* It is out of print and almost impossible to find, but I think it would interest you, because I think you may be related to one of the pooches in the book.

Mary tells me that your ancestry line goes back to the Marquis de Lafayette. Did you know that Dr. Franklin spent some time in Paris? If any of your forebears had been as fetching as you, he certainly would have taken note of them. Ooh-la-la, how he loved the ladies!

I will have to do research to see if Dr. Ben loved dogs as much as the girls. This could be an important clue to the American Revolution, the Declaration of Independence, and the United States Constitution. Do you know what these are? Did you know that I live near the Liberty Bell? Do you even know what a bell is? Oh, poor ZZ, you've so much to learn.

Remember these words: life, liberty, and the dogged pursuit of happiness.

Zeeez, I wonder: do you ever have a little red wine with your dinner? Did you know they say that's why French ladies never get chunky? Please remember, a lady *never* eats from someone else's plate. How rude! If

Peloton does this, he may be in serious need of boyfriend training. This is a very profound topic. You may need to discuss it with Mary or Jim.

By the way, we have lots of restaurants in Philadelphia that cater to dogs, but not of the canine type. Even the French restaurants here, run by frogs (whatever that means), do not cater to pooches.

Do dogs have cake at birthday parties? Did you share, like a well-bred dog? Or was it—as I suspect—all about, "Me, Me, Me, Me, Me?" Get a grip, Z. You may think it's all about you. And sometimes, it well may be. But in the big picture (do you know what that means?) we are only as successful as our relationships with others.

xxoo,

Auntie Ness

Dear Auntie Ness,

I pretty much always share, as long as there is something in it for me. But when there is only one bone, well, certain things simply are not to be shared.

ZZ

Woofs to the Wise:

Certain things simply
are not to be shared.

3

Mani-Pedis and Mothers

Dearest Auntie Ness,

I am so excited about your trip to Seattle. To think that when you get here, I will get my first in-person Diva-in-Training lessons! Mary and Jim can't wait to see you.

Tell me, tell me, what kind of shampoo do you use? I use Johnson's Baby Shampoo. Jim puts it on me in the shower. What kind of toothpaste? Phew, so many details; I think you and I should just play and let Mary worry about the particulars.

I am a pooped pup today. On my Fridays at the dog park, I not only boss around Peloton, but also a bunch of bigger, goofy dogs, mostly males. Whew! Tomorrow is my day off. I always sleep in with Mary, and we snuggle a lot. We let Jim go off and teach yoga. It's the only rest I get all week. Boys sure are high maintenance, know what I mean?

After all, I need my rest, not just sleep. Sleep and rest are different. Humans, I have noticed, don't seem to understand that. I think that you can get lots of sleep, yet not be rested. Resting means to take time to not think about anything. To rest means to be still. I have found that when I get enough rest, I am much smarter and can solve problems much better. When I am rested, outsmarting Peloton comes naturally.

Love,

ZsaZsa

Zees:

Well, Ms. ZsaZsa, do you use conditioner? These airlines are a pest with their regulations. How is a girl to look her best? Baby shampoo is excellent. I am sure Mary has toothpaste. I will concentrate on the other stuff.

Aside from shampoos, does Jim take proper care of your nails? Does he polish them too? I hope he does. It will give you a definite edge and uptick in your already stylish life. My favorite nail color is a shade of very light pink called "Mademoiselle." Like all good things and Bulldogs it is French. In your case, I believe the shade would make you look like a fetching damsel.

Ms. ZZ, should we get mani-pedis? Should we get massages? Should we just walk? I am sure we will have ample opportunity to sip wine.

The countdown begins now!

xxoo,

Ness

Dear Auntie Ness,

Mary wants to know what you take for breakfast in the morning. She wants to make sure that we're stocked up for you. You will just love the breakfast deck of our floating home. It's our favorite place for daytime meals. Then, when it's cocktail time, we all move up to the top deck. I can look down from there on any dogs that might be trying to horn in on my territory and scare them with my barking.

You mentioned nail polish. You would be happy to know that I had my nails painted red for Christmas last year. As a result I received even more compliments than usual. This may become a tradition.

I have done a lot of typing (pawing?), so now I must take a nap.

Love,

ZZ!!!

Dear Z:

I like naps too. In fact, I am going to take one as soon as I finish writing to you. Please tell Mary that oatmeal with dried cherries is my favorite breakfast, and that vodka martinis, straight up with olives are my cocktail of choice. For wine, like dogs, anything French will do, depending on fish or fowl. You are too young to drink, so forget that. Oatmeal, I am sure, would never find its way into your dish. Too messy! You would end up needing another shampoo. And I am still waiting to know what kind of conditioner you prefer.

Hugs & kisses,

Ness

Dearest Auntie Ness,

Personally, I don't use conditioner, but we have loads of it around. Mostly cadged from all the hotels Mary used to visit.

How did you know that Jim does my mani-pedis? He uses this clever gizmo called a Pedipaws. But I really prefer him to use a nail file. Do you want Jim to do your nails too? I know how to ask him so that he usually understands. We could do a spa day!

And a massage, what a good idea! There are places nearby where you could get one. Mary does all of mine, whenever I want. She might give you a massage too, while Jim does your nails. What do you think of that?

Tomorrow is Mother's Day. I am taking Mary for a walk. She is always sad on Mother's Day, and she told me that you might be sad too. Her Mommy seems to have gone away. So did mine, but sometimes I think Mary is my real Mommy, even though she is so much bigger and less hairy than me.

Time for a little nippy-nap.

Love,

ZsaZsa

My Dearest Pooch:

Yes, Mother's Day is a sad one. I even looked at all the Mother's Day cards at Rite Aid and CVS. That's pathetic. But it was something that had to be done. Realize that even if our Moms are not here, they are always in our hearts. They are part of that little voice that continues to talk to us, and we can be glad that it is still there.

We will do mani-pedis, massage, and anything else that makes us beautiful inside and out. Mind you, I will take a pass on Mary and Jim's services. That would be odd, to say the least. But we can go to the spa. Oh, what a good time we will have. You know our Moms would approve.

Your guardian once sent me a cartoon with the caption: "Real Women don't need an excuse to have a mani-pedi." She added her own note: "Since *when* is this news?????" Anyway, dear Miss LaPooch, the countdown continues.

Anon,

Your Ness

Dear Auntie Ness,

I bet that you and Mary were looking at cards at the same time. She also rereads all her former Mother's Day columns, and looks at the book she dedicated to her Mom. She is glad you knew her Mom, and that she knew yours. Mary knew Jim's Mom, too, but she also has disappeared.

Where do all these Mommies go, I wonder?

Moving on to supplies: Mary found a hair conditioner from a swanky hotel and put it right into the "NesSuppliesSatchel." Oh, and she wanted me to mention that she has loads of sunscreen, so don't worry about that. Just bring really comfortable walking shoes, even if they are ugly sneakers. She wears Earth Shoes, but will deny it if you ever breathe a word about it. I don't have any shoes. This is my report *du jour.*

Love,

ZsaZsa

Dear ZsaZsaLa:

Shoes are an extremely important part of a girl's wardrobe. Have you ever heard of Imelda Marcos? She is a very wealthy woman in the Philippines, a long way from Seattle, who at one point had eight closets filled with shoes. Oh, what a woman! She may have been a bit of a dictator (bossy in the extreme), yet her style was superb. This, too, is a lesson. We must find good in everyone, even the ones that seem a tad bit tyrannical.

Please also note this cardinal rule: always try to look your best; you don't know whom you may run into. So Mary may have to pretty up those Earth Shoes and put pink bows and glitter on them. Maybe a Milk Bone motif would look just as fetching. Earth Shoes? I'm a bit horrified. Since I will be with all of you soon, we must give her a style intervention together.

xxoo,

Your Ness

Woofs to the Wise:

Always try to look your best;
you don't know whom you might run into.

4

Gratitude

Dear Auntie Ness,

I am sad today, because you didn't stay longer. You have only been gone for a day, and I miss you. At first I was confused, because I was napping while you were chatting with Mary. I must have slept very deeply. I was so tired after all the socializing, mani-pedis, and walks we took together. You snuck out without my knowing it!

Anyway, I looked for you and found your scent all over the place, but no Auntie Ness! Did you go back to Philadelphia? Can I visit? Is it a long walk? I can go over two miles, if I am sufficiently motivated. That doesn't happen very often. Once, Jim got me to walk halfway around the lake by telling me we were going to Norm's, which is normally only a three-block walk. Well, I can tell you he won't fool me again. We kept walking until my legs gave out, and I made him carry me for a while.

Anyway, what I am trying to say is that I loved having you stay with us. You gave me scratches and cuddles. I enjoyed the treats you gave me. Not to mention all the kisses. I am grateful.

If I can't find my way to Philadelphia, perhaps you will come back here for another visit. I know that you would always be welcome.

Lonesomely,

Your little ZZ

Dear ZsaZsa:

I did not mean to leave without saying a proper good-bye. I must tell you that I only let people and pooches look at me when I feel that I am looking my very best. When you grow up, you will realize that looking good is a woman's prerogative and a condition to be devoutly aspired toward. A wise woman never should be caught unawares.

I am grateful to have spent time with you, and to have had a chance to give you treats and scratches. And cuddling—that is truly a specialty of yours. I am grateful to have a new friend in you. It is especially nice to be able to write back and forth, now that we know what each of us smells and looks like.

I really had the best time. You are a natural hostess, and I have to hand it to you: you always look good. I wonder, do you ever have any bad hair days? I have been having more than my fair share lately.

I miss you already,

Auntie Ness

Dear Auntie Ness,

I think I mostly have good hair. People say I have a heart on my back, but I know my heart is in the right place.

Sometimes the hair on my back stands up, especially if I feel like some pooch or—Dog forbid!—some other creature is trying to horn in on my turf. I simply cannot abide raccoons, squirrels, or beavers. But cats, those I can tolerate perfectly well; I just keep my distance and give them the eye, so they know better than to mess with me.

I wish you could come over later today. We could get another mani-pedi, if you like. Just come back for a little ZsaZsa love.

Licks,

ZZ

Dear ZsaZsa:

I am so lucky to have you as a pen pal. Most of the other people I write to take days to write back. But you always seem to find the time to dash off a few thoughts and ask me a question or two.

I must say that you are giving me a whole new appreciation of gratitude and showing me a whole new dimension, if you will. And that is a very good thing.

You are lucky that you have such loving guardians. Do you ever hear about stray dogs, the ones who have to fend for themselves, scrounging for every bite they eat, or for a dry and warm place to sleep?

You are one lucky little pooch, and you really should be grateful every day. In fact, go give Mary and Jim a little lick right now to show them how grateful you are. Don't wait another minute. And—while it is usually unseemly for a Diva like me to show gratitude this way—please give them a lick for me.

Love to you from your grateful Auntie

Dear Auntie Ness,

You know, that was a great idea you gave me. I just went and gave out a few licks, which they weren't expecting. Usually they have to ask, and I don't always accommodate the request.

Well, this behavior made them so happy that they gave me a little peanut butter, picked me up, and carried me around for quite a while.

Thank you for being such a wise Auntie! I will give them more licks for you all the time.

I love you,

ZZ

5

Achieving Naughtiness with Distinction

Dear AN,

I am confused. Again!

It is nearly holiday time, and Mary says that I am naughty. What does naughty mean? You told me when you visited that you are a "Naughty Diva." Since I want to be just like you, I need you to explain what that means. How do I do it? Do I get more treats? If I am very naughty, can I become a Diva like you? I have heard of Divas who sing, but I am wondering, could there also be barking Divas? Maybe I do not really understand what a Diva is. Can you help me?

XX,

ZZ

Dear ZZ:

Now, ZZ, you little cutie patootie, let me explain a few things.

Holiday time is when a chubby man in a red suit and a white beard takes stock of all the young people and gives them treats. They get the best treats if they are nice. When they are not nice, they get coal. Of course, I get coal all the time. I like coal because I can use it to draw pretty pictures on the sidewalk. I enjoy being very naughty and somewhat devilish. You should ask some of my doctors. Their bedside manners need help and are in great need of repair.

You can tell I am especially mischievous when I have a twinkle in my eye. Do you have eyelashes, by the way? I am definitely a highly evolved woman and a 21st century Diva (always with a capital "D"), although I only sing in the shower.

Now I am going to give you a little historical perspective. Remember, history is how you got to where you are right now. You are likely trolling for treats or romping in the park as I write this.

Singing in the shower is a clue. The first Divas were opera singers, and more often Italian, rather than French. But we can live with that, since the word *Diva* comes from the Italian, meaning a female deity. My heart be still; we are veritable goddesses! In your case, upon completion of your training, you might become a Doggess! Of course, things change, but not human (or canine) nature. Let this be a Woof to the Wise.

Here is what the term *Diva* really means today:

- An extremely talented professional performer or creative talent with little tolerance for incompetence. Therefore, Divas ought to be treated with respect.
- There are, however, some malcontents who interpret the word in a pejorative sense. Let me assure you, little one, that Divas have evolved in the 21st century; we are neither (excuse the Italian) bitches, nor are we high maintenance.
- If we have been properly mentored by the Divas who have come before us, then we pay forward by helping others make the grade. But real Divas remain zealously respectful, thoughtful, and even, on occasion, deferential.
- And of course, we always have fun.

Now frankly, I have never before mentored a pooch on the track toward Divadom, but there is always a first time, and I am willing to give it a go, if you are.

Hugs to you,

Your Diva (High)Ness

Woofs to the Wise:

Things change, but
not human (or canine) nature.

Dear Auntie Ness,

Oh, please take me on. I'll be so good. I'll even teach you how to snorfle, a trick generally confined to French bulldogs. Mary has been teaching me petiquette. In return, I have been demonstrating the art of nonverbal communication.

Jim has been teaching me the rules of soccer, but I choose not to follow most of them. Although it violates some of Mary's petiquette rules, I am teaching him to be alert and look down when walking. I try my best, but he just keeps stepping in it.

In eager anticipation that you will say yes,

ZsaZsa

P.S.: Did you know that Mary has her own mentor? She calls "Tish" Baldrige a First Diva petiquette expert. She has learned some pointers from her Jack Russell terriers that she kept in a White House. Not sure why that is important. But Tish says that:

"A Diva always carries herself as such, and expects to be treated as one the minute she appears in the doorway [I have come by this naturally] and is promptly seated in the position of honor. Treats are welcome provided they
- Are not messy or leak onto other food
- Are easy to transport
- Don't smell bad

"A Diva apologizes selectively. For example, should she squirt something onto someone's shoe, she shows abject misery when that happens. A Diva usually apologizes when and if she is late.

"A Diva does not delve into, or become intrusively curious about, the backgrounds of her companions-of-the-moment or the place where she is being entertained.

"A Diva hangs back when the hostess effusively greets new guests. A Diva waits to shower the new guest with a certain amount of her personal attention."

I have observed that Mary seems not to consider herself a Diva. She clearly does not take this training program as seriously as you and I do. She needs your help too. Perhaps, when I have finished my training, she will want to sign up for this instructional program after all.

Love and Licks,

Z

My Dear ZZ:

It's a deal!

Miss Baldrige is a very wise woman, What she says about Divas is all very true. But the first thing you must know about Divas is that we all have our own unique style of Divadom. I know that Mary does not consider herself a Diva, but believe me, she very much is. Her style may not be identical to mine, but it is complementary. Highly evolved Divas seek harmony in their relationships. I have been fortunate for many years to have had the perfect foil for my mischief as Mary's friend.

You know, in my experience, sometimes people pretend to be nice because they want treats, and that is not a good thing. It is better to be openly naughty than falsely nice. That is a true sign of Divahood. These are my 10 Points on the Road to Diva Naughtiness. Your goal, like mine, is to have a perfect score every day.

10 Points on the Road to Diva Naughtiness

1. Never be mean.

Meanness is so over. One should never laugh at others, especially for a failing that can't be helped. True Divas draw strength from their shortcomings. In your case, you may only stand nine inches tall on your four little feet. You may not be employable as a greeter at Walmart. But your smallness has contributed to your undeniable success soothing patients in Jim's medical practice.

2. Be creative.

Highly evolved Divas are always thinking about new and unexpected ways to use their talents. In your case, always find a new place to hide your ball so that what you do is unexpected, gets attention, and earns treats.

3. Honesty is paramount.

Never lie. If a nasty person (or one without a bedside manner) enters a real naughty Diva's realm, she won't be afraid to growl. But she will do it pleasantly. In your case, utilize all the cuteness you can muster. Then, maybe they will get it when you tell them you are having a bad hair day, or something else they don't want to hear.

4. Communicate smartly.

Highly evolved Divas are never sloppy or hasty in how they communicate. They don't seek attention by barking or with a lot of showy antics. Instead, real Divas force others to pay attention by giving attention to others.

For example, when your ball rolls under the chair, and you can't get at it, don't be obvious and bark like a puppy. Instead, position yourself where you cannot be missed and make eye contact with the most important person in the room. This will force others to pay attention to all your fetching looks and actions.

Now here is the key, Zees. Alternate *your* attention between the person and the ball. It's all about the ball, but you will have made people *think*—and possibly even believe—that this whole thing is about them. Poor fools.

This is rarely the fastest way to gain attention. However, the treats, when you receive them, will give you a far better payoff.

5. Be a gracious host (without sacrificing your treats or naptime).

A Diva knows how to make a guest feel welcome, while also setting limits. Now ZZ, I have heard that when other pooches visit you, you tend to get snarly. This is okay in terms of naughtiness, but you must keep your snarl under control.

For one thing, these guests would not be visiting if they did not care about you or the people who are close to you. Yet, as a Diva-in-Training, you have to let them know what the rules are. In your case, dear ZZ, it is fine to give guests love and licks for a short time; then curl up and take a nap right in front of them. They will understand, because your staff, Mary and Jim, will entertain them.

However, if your staff is not right on hand, then it is important to communicate honestly and smartly. For me, that might sound like, "I'd love to see you. Let's get together for an hour or so on ..." Because you already have set the expectations of your guests, it is entirely appropriate to conclude the visit. Stand up and say something like, "I'm so glad we had some time to visit." But I don't expect guests to give me treats. As a Diva, this is where you trump me.

6. Keep learning, with the bar set high.

A 21st century Diva always tries to learn as many new tricks as she can. She makes up her own. For me, it means never being afraid to ask a question or to admit to what I don't know. For you, it means not being satisfied with your old tricks. I try that myself, and it's a great feeling, especially when I hit 10 on the Diva scale.

For example, instead of just catching the ball, you might bounce it back, then observe the reaction of others. You are now setting the bar high and will undoubtedly get treats for your efforts. You might even be drafted by the Seattle Mariners baseball team as a free agent. If that doesn't happen, take two aspirin and call me in the morning. I will have a word with the Phillies.

And remember one of my favorite sayings: "Good. Better. Best. Never let it rest until the good is better, and the better is best."

7. Don't hold grudges.

A 21st century Diva knows it is easier to ignore someone who has offended you than to create a scene. She cultivates the ability of being *too polite to notice* and activates her "hello-so-good-to-see-you" smile. Mind you, along the way, we have all created scenes. In fact, sometimes they are necessary, to make a point. Yet they require a lot of energy. Holding a grudge is like being in a tornado. Because it saps the energy out of you, no matter what accessories you are wearing—even your Barbara Bush pearls—you will look angry and out of sorts. That's so aging! Divas don't really age, so avoid looking angry, always accessorize, and (only if Mary says you are old enough) wear lipstick and mascara.

So the idea here, dear ZZ, is that you can be far more naughty toward those who have crossed you by simply moving on. Save your energy. That is how one becomes a Diva. This does, I admit, take a lot of practice, and very few of us completely master it.

8. Always find the humor in situations.

And don't be afraid to exploit it. Not everybody can be clever and witty at the same time. But Divas can, because part of being naughty and Diva-like means always watching and listening to the people who teach you. The other part is looking for the connections between those lessons and your real life.

For example, there was a man who everybody said looked like an English bulldog, but he was very witty and wise, and a leader among pooches as well as people in England, another faraway place. His name was Winston Churchill. One night at a dinner party, a nasty guest said to him, "Prime Minister, if I were your wife, I would poison you." Mr. Churchill replied, "If I were your husband, Madame, I would drink it."

9. Always look your best.

Never be without a mani-pedi. There is no excuse for a bad hair day or *eau de canine.* Remember that a Diva is always on display. People want to look at Divas. The smart ones emulate Divas. For example, if running or exercising, a Diva always wears a good sports bra, plus simple, yet elegant jewelry to complement her outfit. To not be so attired means that a Diva does not know or care who she is. A Diva always puts her best paw forward, at the best of times and the worst of times. A Diva is always on display and knows it.

10. Be mischievous with a twinkling eye, a kind heart, and a cool head.

If you achieve this and the preceding nine points, you qualify as a Diva-in-Training, and I will proudly become your mentor, providing treats and tasteful accessories as appropriate.

And that's the way it is done!

Love,

AN

Dear Auntie Ness,

I am going to work hard on all 10 of your points. In fact, from now on I think I'll be going to Norm's with a whole new attitude! But I can tell you that I won't be walking around the lake again to get there; I'll make Jim take me by bus! My dog walker, Annie, takes me on buses all the time.

Heavily influenced by all the wonderful advice you have given me, I sit regally on her lap, so that all the passengers have a better opportunity to admire my DivaNess-in-Training.

Love and Licks,

ZsaZsa

Woofs to the Wise:

Remember these words:
life, liberty, and the dogged pursuit of happiness.

Top Dogs
& New Tricks

6

Being Thankful, Even for Squirrely Gifts

Dear ZsaZsa:

I see by my calendar that it is nearly mid-October. It is your birthday soon, is it not? How do you celebrate your birthdays? Do you go out to dinner? Do you wear your pearls? I wonder if you get to eat any cake. Are you allowed?

Lovingly,

Auntie Ness

Dear Auntie Ness,

Yes, my birthday is soon. This is my favorite time of year. Right after my birthday is Halloween, which I like because I just can't get enough treats. And then there are all the big dinner parties that seem to happen after that. I like being the center of attention.

Of course we have cake at my birthday parties. They are always held at Norm's, for obvious reasons. Plus, I give some of my cake to any other dogs that happen to be sitting around the place.

Right across the street from Norm's there used to be this really great pet store, Railley's, where we got doggie cakes. The owner, Mark, always gave me treats, especially if I danced for him. Peloton does not know how to dance like me; he used to just jump into the display case to go after all the treats. This was like mayhem under glass. Poor Peloton. Sometimes he is so clueless. But then Mark closed his store, and now we have to go a lot farther to find a pet store.

Gotta go now. Jim and I are going to play soccer in the hallway. Sometimes we pass the ball back and forth. He uses his feet, and I use my nose. But what I really like to do is grab the ball with my teeth and run with it; I make him chase after me. He is ready for a nap when we are finished playing. I am sorry we didn't get a chance to play soccer together when you were staying with us, but I guess we just got too busy.

You know, sometimes I get tired waiting around for Mary and Jim to help me type out my notes to you. Maybe there is a keyboard for pooches out there, somewhere ....

Licks and snorfles,
(Do you even know what a snorfle is?)

ZZ

Dear ZEEEEEEEEEEEEEEEEEES:

Stop worrying about your typing. Have you ever read anything typed from an iPhone? It's my favorite new toy, but very trying sometimes. Do you have a cell phone? Shall I get you one for your birthday? A girl must always carry her cell phone and $20, in case of emergencies. In your case, it may be biting emergencies.

It is a good thing that you share your cake with other dogs. It means, my little Diva-in-Training, that you are looking at the big picture and considering others beyond the tip of your little wet nose.

By the way, didn't you mean to say "snore-full"? Proper elocution, carriage, and grammar are important to being a lady. Did you ever walk with a book on your head to learn proper posture? Think about it.

Hmmm…soccer? Well, I am always ready to learn something new. Next time I come out, please teach me. Will I like it? Should I get a lesson or two? I remember playing kickball when I was in school. Is soccer like kickball? Do the players bite each other? Keeping our bodies in shape is as important as keeping our minds in shape, not to mention our stylish demeanor.

Can't wait to see you again.

Loves, licks and maybe
even teeny, tiny little bites,

Auntie Ness

Dear Auntie Ness,

I am losing my sense of humor. Halloween is coming up soon. My pal Maddy, who stays with me when Jim and Mary are away, brought me a present. She was so excited about it. Of course, I was too, until I found out what it was.

Can you believe this? Her gift was a squirrel costume! What was she thinking? *Was* she thinking?

It is just the worst: a gray fuzzy thing, with a stupid-looking acorn between its paws, a great big tail, and a mask with a pudgy face! And of course, she and Mary just *had* to put it on me, *and* they made me walk up and down the dock for all to see. Is that humiliating or what? Suppose Bailey or any other dogs had seen me parading around? Of course, they are so easily confused that they probably would just think, "Oh, Mary's walking a big squirrel on a leash." But who knows?

Am I supposed to be grateful for this embarrassment? I'm so worried about what Maddy might do for my birthday—a gorilla suit? Bat wings? Dog only knows. How can I tell her that I just wish she would stick to the treats? Those are gifts I really like.

L & L,

ZZ

Dear ZZ:

Did you ever think that Maddy just wanted you to experience what it feels like to have a tail? I mean, really ...give her the benefit of the doubt. After all, she did not try to dress you up like a fish, did she?

And yes, I do expect you to thank her and to give her lots of love and kisses, you misguided little pooch. Are you wondering why? Of course you are.

Pay attention: When Maddy picked out the squirrel costume for you, it meant that she was thinking of you with lots of love. She wanted you to take part in the very American tradition of Halloween. She thought you would look adorable. I mean, no squirrel ever looked so good, right? So she spent time, and money, on you.

Remember, she is a student, so money is not so easy to come by as treats are for you. Then she brought it over, all by herself, to present it to you. Think of all the time and attention she lavished on you, just to make you happy and share a special day.

I do see where you are coming from. Playing a squirrel is something of a come-down for an elegant French bulldog such as you. And I doubt that the pudgy face mask did anything to enhance your lovely bone structure. Still, she gave it to you out of love and devotion, and you should be grateful.

Zeez, there are plenty of pooches and people around who go completely unloved and uncared for. They get no loving time or attention, and when you come right down to it, time and attention are the only true gifts we have to give.

You don't have to pretend to be a squirrel for at least another year, if ever again. Meantime, I bet that Maddy will bring you more treats and that she never expects anything in return, except licks and snuggle time. Not a bad deal, if you ask me.

Love,

AN

Woofs to the Wise:

Time and attention are the only
true gifts we have to give.

Dear Auntie Ness,

You don't really expect me to be happy in a squirrel outfit, do you? Seriously.

Okay, I get your point about the gift of time and attention, and enjoying treats in the spirit they are given, even if they are waaaay off the mark. Sometimes you can be so annoying.

You know, every Easter, Jim and I deliver carefully-wrapped homemade doggie treats to the other dogs on the dock and in our apartment building. Mary makes yummy banana and oatmeal cookies, just for pooches. I have caught her and Jim munching on them, too, but I digress.

Everybody is surprised when they open the presents for their pooches. I must admit that it makes me really happy to see their smiles.

I tell you this so that you don't think I am clueless. But I never, ever, will be grateful to be made to look like a squirrel!

Love,

ZZ

ZsaZsa:

Now, while I cannot blame you for being a bit miffed about the squirrel costume, I hope you know enough to always have the good manners to acknowledge a gift that was made with kind intention. Has Mary taught you about thank you notes yet? This is one of her specialties. Especially with your birthday just a few days away, I suggest that you sit at her feet, or in her lap, which might make things a bit more difficult, while she puts pen to paper in her inimitable style.

With Love,

AN

Woofs to the Wise:

Always have the good manners to acknowledge
a gift that was made with kind intention.

Dear Auntie Ness,

As a matter of fact, I have learned a few things about thank you notes from Mary. She helped me write one to Peloton on my own personal stationery. I thanked him once for a dinner date (which provided an excuse for his guardians, Scott and Sheela, to share a meal with Mary and Jim).

Not only that, but I have received a few thank you notes for gifts I gave. Mary and Jim's dogdaughter Dani, whom I love, had her friend Joy come out and stay with me for a few days. It might not surprise you to know that Joy sent me a thank you note for allowing this to happen, and for allowing her to give me massages and hugs. Oh, and she thanked me for the love and licks I gave her.

So I know that thank you notes work both ways: you thank others, and they thank you. Plus you get mail. That may not be as good as treats, but it isn't half bad either.

I just can't get enthusiastic about sending a thank you note for a squirrel outfit. Instead, if I am extra nice to Maddy, and wear my best pearls when I am around her, I am hoping she might get me something really useful for my next birthday, like a costume befitting The Right Honorable ZsaZsa LaPooch, Dowager Countess of the Seattle Floating Manor.

Does that show you what a good learner I am?

I love you, Auntie Ness. You really are beginning to understand me.

ZZ

Dear Little One:

I am speechless. You are getting quite the education.

AN

7

Some Days Are Better Than Others

Dear Auntie Ness,

My fifth birthday was today. It was miserable. I thought it would be really special and fun, and everyone would make a big fuss over me. I was expecting so many scratches and treats that I could hardly stand it.

That didn't happen. First, I had to hang around and wait for someone to take me out to play. After Mary took me potty early, she headed to her office. I didn't see her for hours. Meanwhile, Jim was working too. Didn't they know that this was my birthday? Didn't they have any idea that today was supposed to be special and all about making *me* happy?

It got worse. After waiting until this afternoon to play, Mary finally got her priorities straight. She was very enthusiastic, promised me treats, and said she'd take me to Norm's for a birthday Happy Hour. She smiled and told me how much she loves me.

But really, am I supposed to fall for this? A little too late if you ask me.

Now, we did eventually have a little fun. We went to the funeral home. I put the "fun" in funeral home, because that's where I like to play fetch on the lawn. Do you think I am strange because I like to play at a funeral home? They keep the lawn nice and clean there, so when I roll over, I don't get all dirty.

Anyway, after funeral home playtime, we went to the UPS store to send something to one of Mary's friends. I did not mind much—even if she was again making my day all about her—I was somewhat desperate for attention by that point. So it helped that Stephen, who runs the place, gave me scratches and treats.

Finally, we went to Norm's. I was really juicing up for some calamari, my favorite. But can you believe it? Norm's was closed for cleaning!

Well, this was just too much. Don't they understand that I needed a snort (or at least a snorfle) on my birthday, plus a few canines hanging around for me to supervise? And don't you think that Mary, who is supposed to know all about etiquette and dining out and stuff, should have taken the time to be certain they were open so she could entertain me, her special guest of honor?

This was a special day all right—for all the wrong reasons. I didn't like it one bit and couldn't wait for it to be over. The minute I got home, I went straight to my office under the bed, to be by myself and sulk. I only just decided to come out and write to you because I hoped you would understand.

But then I remembered. *You* did not send me a birthday card, a present, or even call me. My cousin Daisy—she is a beagle puppy who lives with Mary's cousins Kate and Pam on the East Coast—sent me a card. And she hasn't even met me! Even clueless Peloton had a present for me: some pretty and tasty treats were waiting outside my door this morning. But not you. Are you not my Auntie anymore?

What gives?

ZZ

Dearest ZsaZsaLa:

Get a grip. Okay, so it was your birthday. Things did not pan out the way you wanted. Let me tell you, cutie paw-tootie, even though I am a Diva, I *always* get myself into trouble when I expect people to react to things exactly the way I would. We are all different, and that is a good thing.

Let me tell you something else. Sometimes, the gifts people give you are hideous. I admit I've had annoying birthdays myself. But when you expect others to do things your way all the time, you rob them of the joy of giving. I promise you this: if you look for the positive in situations and people, the positive will find you.

Tell me, have you given as much thought to what went right with your birthday? For example, you might consider that your day began beautifully with a gift from Peloton, your true love and best friend for your whole life. Lots of people would envy that! You also might consider that you got a card from Daisy, who admires and respects you.

And why are you dismissing the fact that Mary told you how much she loves you? That was a nice thing. How can you berate Dr. Jim? He was working so that he could provide you with a lifetime of treats. And how can you call Peloton clueless when *you* miss the biggest point of all—that birthdays give other people the chance to tell you they are glad to be part of your life?

Also, you should know that I did not send you a card or a present because I have been quite sick, which is really irritating. I am frustrated to have not been able to get out. As a matter of fact, I have been in the hospital, where I also "celebrated" my birthday. As you can imagine, I woke up that morning feeling mighty discouraged to be there. How would you like to be poked and prodded and stuck with needles all day? And then to not even be able to enjoy birthday treats when you got them? Ugh.

While I was in the hospital, some of my dearest pals came to the hospital to celebrate my birthday. They brought me cake, and they sang to me. And you know what? That's when I really got it. Birthdays are about letting others love us the best way they can.

I am not sure how many more birthdays I will have, ZsaZsaLa. None of us knows for sure how many more birthdays we have left. But I am sure that every single day is a gift. Somehow, every single day, I get to love and to be loved.

So take that and chew on it.

And cut Mary a break. Nobody makes reservations for Happy Hour.

Love,

Auntie Ness

Woofs to the Wise:

If you look for the positive in situations
and people, the positive will find you.

My Dear Auntie Ness,

I have a hang-dog look on my face and, if I had anything like a real tail, it would be between my legs. I did not know that you were in the hospital. I used to go with Dr. Jim to cuddle with his patients at his office. My cuteness made them feel more relaxed.

Maybe I should come to Philadelphia and sit on your hospital bed. I'll even let you scratch me in all the right places. Then when you're all better, you can come back to Seattle to play soccer with me. What do you say?

You know, I had something very scary happen to me just a few weeks ago. Jim and I went to the beach. We were playing with my rubber stick. Because I am a bulldog and hate to let go of anything, I clamped down with my jaws for all I was worth. So, as he often does, Jim lifted me up by the stick, and I held onto the other end.

The stick slipped out of my mouth and I fell, probably almost two feet. I hit my back on a concrete dock support and landed on my side on the sand. I thought I was okay, but then, when one of the neighbors walked by and bent over to scratch me, I yelped in pain. A little later, I started shaking uncontrollably.

Jim and Mary were worried, but they couldn't figure out exactly what the problem was. I really did not feel like eating or drinking unless they helped me. I yelped a few more times, and it really hurt to walk, although I was sort of able to do it.

They brought me to see the doctor. I don't like doctors to begin with—except, of course, Dr. Jim—and this one poked and prodded me, and twisted me and turned me. It was not pleasant. And frankly, I felt a lot better as soon as we left the doctor's, mostly just happy to get out of there. So I know exactly what you mean. Being sick is very frustrating and irritating.

To make matters worse, Jim and Mary started giving me a different kind of peanut butter. This stuff made me feel sleepy and all relaxed. Don't get me wrong. I really like peanut butter. I like to sleep. And I'm relaxed most of the time anyway. But this was a bit much! I couldn't even offset it with a little "hair of the dog."

But Peloton did send me some delicious frosted treats and a picture of himself looking dejected and sad because I wasn't there. It was a pretty scary few days. It took a long time to get back to myself again. I am still healing, but I am almost ready to start going up stairs again.

I know you will be up and very soon chasing your tail, which, sigh, I will never be able to do, for obvious reasons. Then you can get back to teaching me how to be a Diva just like you.

Love,

ZsaZsa!!!

Dear ZsaZsa:

Well, what a tale to tell, even though you don't have much of one to speak of … if you get my drift!

I am glad you are on the mend. You are one lucky pooch; it could have been much worse. What do we say about playing dangerous games? Never, never, never.

Enjoy those peanut butter treats. Stay calm. You will get plenty of attention, even more than usual. I understand how traumatic this must have been for you, as well as for Jim and Mary. Now that you are on the mend, take care!

xxoo,

Your Auntie Ness

Dear Auntie Ness,

You are the only person to ever say to me, "What a tale." Most big people don't think I even have one at all! One snide type asked my guardians whether they had my tail bobbed, whatever that means. He has a dog named Bob with a long tail. But I could put him in his place sure enough, you betcha. I may not have a tail, but I do have an attitude.

I am much better; I went up a few stairs today and ran a little bit too. My guardians were upset about me; I tried to tell them that I was going to get better, but I wasn't sure enough to press the point. (By the way, even though I am officially classified by the American Kennel Club as a "nonsporting dog," I do know how to point.)

I promise I will be more careful in the future. You take care of yourself too.

Love to you, Auntie Ness
(and thanks for not scolding Jim),

ZZ

P.S.: Guess what? Last night I got to see Peloton and my heart went pitta-pat. We played for a tiny bit, and then I just laid down on the floor. But he inspires me to get better, and, by Dog, I will!

8

Neighbors, and How to Be a Good One

Dear Auntie Ness,

Something has happened around here that really has me upset, and, frankly, I don't know what to do about it. This is really a revolting development.

I had been minding my own business and the business of everybody else in the neighborhood (as best I can) and what do I find, to my absolute horror, but a *new puppy* in the community.

The worst thing is that this little pup—with the longest, dumbest ears I have ever seen—toddles by my front door more times each day than I can shake a paw at. And everybody acts like I'm supposed to be nice to this fledgling Fido.

His name is Andre, and he is something called a Bassett hound. He is always trying to get up close and lick me. Frankly, he has not earned his spots yet. After all, I was here first!

Well, actually Bailey was here first, but I have invested a great deal of time in protecting our community from intruders. Bailey, on the other hand, just worries about her own house. (Most people think I was just sunning myself ... but I always keep one eye open. You just never know who or what might try to sneak by.)

Anyway, I don't know whether to consider this Andre an intruder who must be driven out, or a canine that must simply be tolerated. The odds of our becoming good friends are very small. After all, I have my boyfriend Peloton, and I am fiercely loyal to him. And I have my best girlfriend Bailey. And then there is the elder statesman Sonny, a pug; I tolerate him.

Everybody wants us to be friends, and all they talk about is how adorable Andre is. Hrrumph. Nobody asked *me* if he's adorable.

To make matters worse, even Mary and Jim are fussing over this young upstart—right in front of me, no less! Do you think I need to try to be even cuter to get their attention back? I think they have their priorities all wrong these days.

Have you ever been in a situation like this? What did you do? Help! This could develop into a full-fledged turf war.

Love,

ZsaZsaLa

Ah, dearest ZsaZsaLa:

This is jealousy, I am afraid to say. It's like being the oldest child, and then along comes a baby who diverts all the attention. Understand that I think you are the cutest, sweetest, and best of everything. But there is a lesson here.

ZZ, dearest, as hard as this is to hear, you may have to learn to *share*. You have to acknowledge that there are others who are as cute as you, but cute in a different way; as smart as you, but smart in a different way.

Now, just think of the power you could have over the entire turf if you decided to become friends with this interloper—ah, I mean newcomer.

Do something nice for the newcomer. Wag your tail. Ask him to go to the store with you for a treat. If you show him the ropes, you will have a new best friend and you will be able to retain control of the situation. You will remain the alpha dog of cuteness ... but with a partner.

Just remember, ZZ dearest, puppyhood cuteness is only fleeting. You, of course, have retained all your good looks as well as your personality. Be charitable to the new one. Have him become dependent on you, and you can be the boss of him.

Don't show this email to Mary. She may get upset about your being the boss of someone, when your primary job is to cuddle.

Let me know how it goes,

Your Ness

AN,

I am thinking about not being your friend for a day or so. Do you want to know why? Well, let me tell you, I do not think it is one bit nice to make fun of someone's disability. You told me to "Wag your *tail*." Why would you say such a thing to me, after all these months? After I jumped up and sat on your lap and gave you kisses and everything? After all that advice I gave you about what to bring to Seattle?

You have spent time with me. You know full well that I cannot "wag my tail." I hardly have a tail at all, and it only works when I go you-know-what. I have to show my emotions with my eyes, ears, and body language. You know that. I am really hurt.

I think you have forgotten that I am not like other dogs. I am perfectly aware that the way you look on the outside reflects what's going on inside.

Still, I guess the rest of what you said makes a lot of sense, especially about how I can be the boss of little Andre. So I guess you can be sure I still love my Auntie Ness.

Your ZZ

P.S.: I heard Mary tell Jim that you were shopping for treats that they called antiques. Aren't they old things? I don't like old treats. I nudge them aside with my nose if they sit in my bowl for too long. How old does a treat need to be before it is called antique?

Woofs to the Wise:

The way you look on the outside
reflects what's going on inside.

Dear Zzzzzeeeeeeeees:

Apologies. I think of you as a complete dog. No offense.
A treat is antique at two days old; a piece of furniture at 100 years; and a person whenever they get cranky.

xxoo,

Your Ness

Oh Auntie Ness,

You are so wise. I know I can always count on you to clue me in about stuff. Of course I accept your apology.

I must admit that I have been known to get cranky when Jim and Mary tell me they are going out for a while and that I am "in charge." I really do not like all that responsibility, and especially the consequent lack of attention. I let them know by withholding all eye contact. Yet I don't think this qualifies me as an antique, since most of the time I am actually quite pleasant.

Licks,

Your ZZ

Decisions

Dear Auntie Ness,

I am frustrated. Today I went for a walk with Jim. We came to a crosswalk, and I just could not decide which way I wanted to go. So I put my paws down and sat for a while to make up my mind.

This did not go over well with Jim. He growled something about needing to get on with the day. (I thought I was the only one who got to growl … but I digress.) This did nothing to move me, of course. I'm stubborn and proud of it. Comes from being French.

Still, how do you know which way to go when you cannot decide? Does this ever happen to you?

Love,

ZZ

Dearest ZsaZsa:

Indecision is part of every thinking being's life. That is because we consider different points of view. It goes way beyond which way we will garner the most or the best treats. Have you ever considered that, my little cutie patootie?

Yes, of course I have trouble deciding things sometimes. However, unless I am totally lost, this usually does not occur at busy intersections. Sometimes the decision is a matter of what bling to wear that day, or what color my mani-pedi should be. Other times the decisions are harder because the consequences last much longer than nail polish.

Occasionally, though, I am faced with decisions that leave me feeling like I am frozen at the crosswalk. Zeeeez, I do not have all the answers. Nobody does, and I guess that's because we are not supposed to. This is how I make most of my big decisions. Perhaps these steps will help you lead a better dog's life:

Decision Making with Diva-Ness

- First, ask yourself what you really want to do.
- Then ask yourself if what you want is good for you.
- Think about if, and how, your decision will affect other people, especially people you love.

- Imagine what life will be like if you don't do what you really want. Ask yourself if you can handle that.
- When you are really stuck, toss a coin.

Now that I think of it, I realize that last guideline might be a challenge, if you try it with your paws. Still, it seems to me that once we do our best to decide, we need to appreciate the journey, whichever direction it takes us.

Love,

Auntie Ness

Dear AN,

Once, I ran after a flock of pigeons by crossing four lanes of traffic during rush hour, with Jim chasing after me. He scolded me and told me to never do anything like that again. I think that might be why I have a hard time making up my mind at intersections. I want to chase the pigeons, but I don't want to be scolded. Maybe you could explain it to Mary and Jim. They just think it's cute to see me so indecisive.

ZZ

Dear ZZ:

I think you hit the nail on the head here. Which isn't easy to do when you can't grip a hammer. Your thought processes really amaze me.

AN

Dear Auntie,

Thank you for that. Sometimes I amaze myself too!

Now that I am a bigger girl, Mary and Jim choose safe places to let me go off-leash. Often, I choose to follow. At other times, when I know where I'm going and what I want to do, I even take the lead. I tear around the grassy knoll, play tug-of-war, and bounce balls off my nose to Jim or Mary. Having a plan helps me get my priorities in order.

By the way, I made a decision about that squirrel costume. Jim tried to get me to wear it on Halloween, but I hid in my office under the bed and refused to come out. I decided to forgo the whole Halloween thing. It's far better for me to give up the treats this time around in order to preserve my dignity. He got the message, and I got my treats the next day!

Licks and Hugs,

ZZ

Table Manners

Dear AN,

I have been hearing talk about Thanksgiving again. My boyfriend and his guardians usually spend it with us. Last year we went to their house. This year it is our turn.

Here's the thing: I have not let Peloton into our place for some time now. In fact, I don't think I will ever let him into our house again. Never. He eats like a maniac! He heads directly to my food, and I cannot get near my own bowl. To make things worse, he is sloppy. When he eats, he looks like a vacuum cleaner on four paws. He even chipped my favorite food bowl!

So, Auntie Ness, I'm warning you now; get ready to hear Jim and Mary complain about what a bad hostess I am. They keep telling me to remember that Peloton and I have loved each other for five years. But I say, "Enough is enough!" We are domesticated canines, after all, not pigs.

Help!

Your ZZ

Ah, little ZsaZsaLa:

Mary and Jim are right. You should love Peloton in spite of his faults and be loyal to him even though he clearly is clueless. You know, Zeeeez, I have two important considerations for you to ask yourself.

First of all, are you setting a good example yourself, or are you dropping down to his level? You know, Z, we really only learn from what we see others do. So don't bitch to me (sorry ... could not resist) about Peloton's bad behavior unless you hold yourself to the same high standards you set for him.

Secondly, my little four-footed friend, do you really think that Peloton is the only such offender? Let me assure you that two-footed creatures eat like pigs too, more often than I care to admit. And, unfortunately for them, they get blocked from lots of important opportunities as a result: jobs, schools, clubs, you name it.

Sadly for them, humans are not as good at communicating clearly as you are, ZZ, so nobody ever tells them the real reason they are not achieving their goals. They just go on making the same mistakes and getting the same responses. It is not fair, but it is real life.

You should feel proud that people love to come to your Thanksgiving dinner. It means you make them feel welcome. I am counting on you to include Peloton, Zeeez. Welcoming him, and all his faults, shows that you love to share the best of life's treats with each other.

Peloton can learn, not only from being around you, but also by observing Jim and Mary. They are models of good table manners. People and pooches can show their guests, and each other, how much they are appreciated through their behavior, not just through the food on the table. Just by watching others, they'll see

- How to use knives, forks, spoons, and napkins correctly.
- Not to eat too slowly or too fast.
- Not to bark or talk with food in their mouths.
- Not to season food before they taste it. (What a slap in the snoot that is to the cook who spent lots of time and energy to prepare the food.)
- Not to text at the table.
- How to sit up straight.
- How to ensure everybody is included in the conversation.

So do not give up on Peloton, ZZ. You have a lot to teach him, and he never gives up on you.

Love to you,

Auntie

Dear Auntie Ness,

Well, okay about Peloton. I am not about to give up on him. I'll just do my best to ensure that Thanksgiving dinner is always at his place, not ours.

But let me tell you about something else that kind of bothers me. There are rare occasions when Mary and Jim decide to go out for dinner and bring me along, even though they may have decided not to go to Norm's. Well, when that happens, we must eat outside. Norm's is the only place I know where dogs are allowed inside. You can imagine how insulted I feel not to be allowed inside any other restaurants. I am very well-mannered as you have seen.

But anyway, there we sit, at a table out on the sidewalk. I sit or lie down, good as gold. If I manage to attract the attention of the waiter, I might get a bowl of water. And of course Jim, that old softy, always sneaks a nibble my way when he thinks nobody is looking.

So there I am, more or less minding my own business, which is all about subtly cadging a little extra protein, when, all too often, passers-by stop and interrupt our dinner.

They say the usual things, like "OMD," or "What kind of dog is that?" Or, even worse, "Can I pet your dog?" This always seems to happen when both Jim and Mary have mouths full of food. So they kind of leave it to me to answer for them by looking especially lovable, when all I want to do is give Jim the secret signal to slip me another scrap.

Should I wear a little sign on my back to warn these people off, something like this:

"Kindly walk on by; serious business at hand here" or "How would you like it if you couldn't eat your dinner without unwarranted interruptions?"

I mean, you wouldn't want me to forgo accompanying my guardians, would you? Don't you think they are happier when we go out as a family, instead of leaving me home, all blue and alone?

Love and Licks,

ZsaZsa

ZZ:

You may have something there. You could start a new trend for pooches at sidewalk tables. Perhaps you could patent the concept of sandwich boards for dining dogs. Let me clue you in here. What you make of your talents is your gift to God. And we all know what that *really* means.

AN

Woofs to the Wise:

What you make of your talents
is your gift to God.

11

Parties

Dear Auntie,

Whew! Am I exhausted today! Mary and Jim had a party last night. This is the season for it, and I was so busy. It's always that way with parties. First, I have to greet everybody who comes. Then I have to let every-one have a chance to pet and scratch me. This takes up most of my party time because I don't want anyone to feel rushed while lavishing attention on me.

Then, when the food comes out (my favorite part), I have to station myself just right so that people notice me, should they happen to have any scraps to pass my way. I have to be careful to appear as though I am not begging. This requires a careful mix of looking both attentive and like I could care less.

This is all quite tiring; it cuts into my normal daily requirement of at least twenty hours sleep. Frankly, the day after, I am not good for much. I don't even feel like playing soccer or "find the hidden ball." Do you think I am overextending myself at parties? Am I violating the

Rules of Diva-Ness by staying underfoot throughout the event? Should I slip off somewhere to take a nap? Do you think I sleep too much? I really need your help on this matter.

Imploringly,

ZZ

Dear Zips:

The answer is really quite simple:

Take charge. Remember whose place it is. When you have guests, you set certain guidelines.

For instance, after an agreed-upon length of time, go to the door, and start whining. Do your usual tricks to make it perfectly clear that you need to go outside, even if you really don't. Look from one guest to the door; then look at another. Get it? One would hope that someone would figure out that there is a connection between your need to go outside and theirs.

If you time it just right, one guest's announcement that she needs to say goodnight will spread like wildfire. Soon they will all be rushing out the door, leaving you in peace. You can just go straight to your bed (or, more likely, Mary and Jim's) and nap until you are really ready to go. Sooner or later, Jim and Mary will come to realize who really is in charge!

Keep those emails coming, girl,

AN

12

House Calls

Dear Auntie Ness,

I have a question: How do you handle yourself when someone shows up unannounced? I ask because the other day Jim showed up after his yoga class with a friend in tow. It totally surprised Mary. Now she handled it with her usual aplomb, but I know when things aren't right with either of my guardians. I did what I could do to cheer her up: let her scratch me while I turned on my back with my legs up. Sure enough, after the person left, she got sharp with Jim. Then I had to console him by letting him pet me.

I don't ever create problems like this, because I won't let any dogs in—not even Peloton. So I ask you, my dear Auntie N, how do you handle it when people show up unexpectedly? Do you pretend you are not home? You should leave your door open all the time. That way, if I ever find myself in Philadelphia, I can easily barge in on you.

Lots of Licks,

ZZ

Dear ZZ:

Leave my door open? Barge in on me? Are you kidding? Get over it. Now.

Much as I dislike taking sides in other people's spats, I have to say that Mary had every right to be cranky when Jim arrived with an unexpected guest. I doubt that I would have been so polite. In fact, I probably would have said, with a faint and feigned smile, "I was just dashing out the door. Nice to see you. So sorry there's no time for a visit."

Obviously, if they caught me in my PJ's, that line would never do. I would have improvised something like, "I was just jumping into the shower so I can be on time for my appointment in half an hour." Only the truly clueless would miss those messages.

Now, Zeez, I must tell you about a tradition that has fallen out of practice, but never should have: the "calling card." We are going back a couple centuries here, when ladies of the house were pretty much stuck there. Nevertheless, "at home" hours were specifically stated and observed. This gave the hostess fair notice that callers might show up, and she would be ready for them: dressed, accessorized, moisturized, coiffed, and bearing plenty of tasty treats.

In turn, the callers also showed up ready for a visit. Their responsibility included being at the ready with conversation starters. We call these "talking points" today.

And, for the very well-to-do, there was "staff" to bring visitors' calling cards to the hostess on a tray, so as not to catch her completely off guard. Nowadays, receptionists and doormen handle this function.

Incidentally, these traditions were prior to the advent of Jehovah's Witnesses. They are religiously unconcerned with calling cards, invitations, or taking a hint that the visit is over.

So much for my history lesson *du jour*, ZsaZsaLa. Whether or not you agree with my point of view, let me get to my bottom line: Don't dare barge in on me unexpectedly. And if you do, take the hint and high-tail it out of there.

Love,

AN

Dear Auntie Ness,

Now it is my turn to register shock and not a little disappointment. First, again with the tail jokes?

But more importantly, I think what you mean to say is that you dislike *unwelcome* visitors. There is a big difference between an unwelcome visitor and an uninvited guest. For instance, a neighbor's cat might choose to leap onto the second floor porch and invite herself in. This has happened to us on more than one occasion. What would be the point of lecturing to such an interloper about visiting hours and calling cards?

I'll give you another example: sometimes, we drop in unannounced on Peloton and his guardians, Scott and Sheela. And sometimes they knock on our door without warning. If things work out, we have a little romp; if not, they try knocking some other time. What's wrong with that?

Love to you,

ZZ

Dear ZZ:

Have I invested too much faith in your civil sensi-
bilities? Perhaps you, Peloton, and all your guardians
have an open-door policy about visiting, because you
consider each other family. In any case, the fact is that
Scott, Sheela, Jim, and Mary all function as your "staff."
Thus, when you two pooches get together, you become
the entertainment, and your guardians are not obligated
to be charming, dress up, accessorize, or even moisturize.

Perhaps Jehovah's Witnesses should take lessons
from you.

Love,

AN

Dear Auntie Ness,

I think that I now have reached that point in my life where I should have calling cards of my very own. I already have correspondence cards with my image on them. But they require more time and patience than I usually have. I mean, what if I just want to let somebody know that I paid a visit?

For instance, this morning I went to see Peloton, but after going over to his house and knocking on the door, he was not there and nobody was home. Should I have to go through all this trouble for nothing? I wished I could have left a little card, the way Mary and Jim do.

I am now thinking about something simple: just my name and email address. Mary says that you know a lot about graphics and art. What's graphics? I know what art is (after all, I have had my portrait painted several times—twice by Oatley and twice by Jim's yoga student, Emily Kane).

Please tell me your thoughts. I never would make such a bold move without asking you first.

Love,

Your ZsaZsaLa

Ah, my dear Zeeeeeeeeeees:

Calling cards for a pooch?

How delightful. How Victorian. (Some Victorians used small photographic cards as business cards. That is old technology.) Today, humans in the work world call them business cards. It's a way to market yourself.

Okay, let's get busy: What is your brand? How do you present yourself to people? What is the buzzword that you want people to remember when they meet you? It should be different and stand out.

If you said *cute*, you might have too much competition.

It seems to me that, in looking over our extraordinary correspondence, the word *treats* comes to mind. You ask for treats. You love treats. When you visit, it is a treat for those who see you.

I have it! I think your business card should be in the shape of your favorite treat. (If we can add Sniff-O-Rama to the card, that would be a plus for some of your four-legged friends, who are not as highly evolved and may not be able to read.)

So let's see what you would put on your business card:

- Your name
- Your email address
- Your cell phone number (You don't have a cell phone. We can scratch that.)

How about a tag line:

> *Zsa Zsa LaPooch says: Bring on the treats!*

Let's discuss further.

xxoo,

Auntie Ness

Dear Auntie Ness,

You know, I think that's just the ticket! *ZsaZsa LaPooch says: Bring on the Treats!* ought to be just perfect. I'll have Jim make one up on the computer. I'll try it on Peloton and see what happens ...

[Paws]

... well, that didn't work. Peloton will not bring on the treats unless he gets plenty for himself. But, as long as we both get them, one at a time, he will share. So maybe the card should say:

Bring on enough treats to go around.

After all, it seems as if there should be more than enough treats for everybody.

We really come up with some good stuff, don't we, you and I?

Your teammate,

ZZ

Dear Little Miss:

Although most teams would only allow you to participate as a mascot, I do consider you a full-fledged miniature Diva-in-Training, if that helps. And you are right about the good stuff!

Licks at you
(I can't believe I am writing this.),

AN

13

Forgiveness

Dear Auntie,

I have been thinking about what you said about being a good host to Peloton, and how Mary, Jim, and I can be models of better behavior for him. But then you suggested I allow Peloton back into the apartment for dinner. You implied that I wouldn't be a good host otherwise.

Well, I thought and thought about this last part. I thought so much that I had to lie down a while to recover from all that thinking. I even had a dream about Peloton eating the whole meal, before anyone else got so much as a taste. When I woke up, I was so upset I had to go over to my bowl to see if there was anything left in it! You know that Jim and Mary almost always leave food in my bowl and let me decide when to eat (usually after I run out of human food alternatives).

Anyway, the food was still there. And I realized that my worries were all in my head. Next thing I know Peloton came by with Scott, who shrewdly *tricked* me into letting Peloton in by carrying Peloton across the threshold. (No, they are not married.)

Well, what was a well-bred pooch like me to do? Scott put Peloton down, and, of course, he ran right for my food bowl. But Mary had anticipated this and put it out of his reach, which means on top of the cabinets.

Then Peloton rushed around and noticed an old bone. Mary had left it there. (You know, I think she was in on the whole thing from the start.) Anyway, Peloton plunked himself down and proceeded to gnaw away. Then Scott gave me lots of love and attention.

When Peloton finished chewing, I let him sniff around my toy basket. Then, just like old times, we rough-housed a bit. We peacefully coexisted after that for over an hour. When it was time for Scott to leave, he picked Peloton up, and Jim put my harness on and we walked together down the hall. I even let Peloton give me a little kiss.

I can tell you, it was pretty exhausting making sure this crazy friend of mine didn't overstep his place. Yet I was kind of proud of my self-restraint.

Maybe I will let him in again, after all.

Aren't you just a little bit proud of your ZsaZsaLa? Admit it.

ZZ

Dear ZZ:

First off, I am more than a little bit proud of you. Almost always. I think you already know you will be really glad to let Peloton in for a special holiday meal.

So what is the lesson here, ZsaZsaLa? I think it's about forgiveness. Now, to be honest, I have never been big on forgiveness myself. That's because I used to think forgiving meant, "Sure, bring it on again. Hurt me again. Go ahead and walk all over me—with cleats." And that definition of forgiveness is unworthy of a Diva, especially a 21st century Diva like myself.

But enlightened Divas are always learning, and I have learned a different way to think about forgiveness. Let me share it with you, because you might be happier when you get it. I know I am.

The Enlightened Diva's Guide to Forgiveness

Forgiving someone does not mean you let him off the hook. It just means you are willing to understand why the person who offended you behaved the way he did.

So, my little darling, in the case of Peloton, it's easy to see why he barges into your house and devours all your food. Food is his big motivator. This is true of many males. Their other big motivator is, well, you are too young to understand. And I digress.

But who knows? Maybe Peloton has an eating disorder. Maybe his guardians do not feed him food as tasty as yours. When I was your age, I used to go to my neighbor's house and ask to eat there; I liked the way they made mashed potatoes. I thought they tasted better than my mom's. So, Zeez, are you beginning to understand?

Forgiving someone means being able to let go of your own anger and resentment so that you can move forward.

In your case, Zeez, don't you feel better now that you are not wasting your precious energy all riled up, with your hackles standing on end? You see, ZZ, forgiving Peloton really is a gift to yourself, because you get your energy back. In some ways, forgiving the offender means that you outsmarted him. Don't you just love that idea?

The bottom line is this: You, Peloton, and everyone at a special occasion, perhaps a meal in your home, will have a better time if you let Peloton back in for the celebration. I think you will be very thankful that you have him as your very best friend, which is a lot more important than who gets both drumsticks. And remember you always drink all his water when you visit his place, and he never growls when you do that.

Love,

Your Ness

Dear AN:

I remember what you said about being a good host and making sure that guests (the invited kind) enjoy themselves. Well, I will forgive Peloton his many past transgressions and see what happens this Thanksgiving. But I have my doubts.

ZZ

Woofs to the Wise:

A host's primary concern is to
see that guests enjoy themselves.

Work Like a Dog

14

Keeping Life in Perspective

Zees:

You may recall, when you first wrote, that I mentioned the importance of introducing oneself properly. That is especially important when promoting yourself and your career. So here is my new bio, LaPooch. Remember the first line is the most important:

Nessa Forman, a Diva in her own "write," is honored to mentor aspiring Divas-in-Training in her third act of life. She made her debut as Arts & Leisure Editor at her beloved "Philadelphia Bulletin" newspaper.

Her second act was long and action-packed as VP of Communications at WHYY, a leading public TV, radio, and online content provider in the "City of Diva-ly Love."

Upon her recent "retirement," Nessa opened Act III as communications consultant and an active leader in the city she loves most. Offstage, she is currently coauthoring a book on civility and creating successful relationships in the workplace and in life.

Please send me your bio. After all, turnabout is fair play. Show me that you now know what a bio is.

xxoo,

Your Auntie Ness

Dearest Auntie Ness,

Of course I know what a bio is! What do you think I am? A dumb dog? After having yours read to me, I worked on mine; here is what I came up with. I know it is pretty short, but remember that I am only five:

ZsaZsa LaPooch is recreational therapist for The Mitchell Organization. Prior to accepting this position, she was an amateur therapy dog for the surgical practice of James K. Weber, MD. There, she was responsible for greeting and soothing all patients and their families, in the office and in the hospital. She is the product of a very happy puppyhood.

Tell me if you think this is complete enough. It seems that I should have more to say.

Love,

ZZ

My dear Ms. Hoochie-Koochie-Poochie:

This is only the beginning of your résumé! Even now it is impressive. It clearly shows that you are dedicated to serving others.

AN

Ah, Auntie N,

You are so wise! I really did not put my bio into full perspective. I was too much in awe of yours. That's about all for now, dear Auntie, except to say that I love you,

ZsaZsa!

15

Getting Names Right

Dear Auntie Ness,

What is it about my name that is so confusing? Some people call me "Cha-Cha," others say "Za-Za." It seems as if no matter what Mary or Jim do to correct these "egregious mispronunciations" (as Jim calls them; he likes to use big words), they never get it right. Now there is even a Hotel ZaZa in Houston! Can you believe it?

Do all these people have a hearing problem? Or a speech defect? I know that some names are harder than others to remember, but ZsaZsa seems like it should be memorable, don't you think?

What do you do to remember tough names? I remember people and pooches best by their smell. Do big people have any kind of sniffing-recognition ability?

Licks to you,

ZZ

Dear ZsaZsa:

Even though you are French, you should perhaps only socialize with Hungarians. They might not know the difference, and all of them certainly would get your name right.

Shakespeare said, "What's in a name? A rose by any other name would smell as sweet." Easy for him to say. "Rose" is a simple, one-syllable name. Who could miss?

Probably the best explanation why people don't say your name right is that they are not listening; they are so enchanted with your adorable visage that they have no interest in anything your guardians have to say. Hence, the ongoing and annoying errors.

It's time for a true confession, Zeeez. (Did I pronounce that right?) I do not always get names correct. I also forget names, even though I have a good memory in general. When I know that I am in name pronunciation or facial-recognition trouble, I resort to something about which you are an expert—tricks.

If someone tells me his name and I don't get how to say it, I will say, "Would you mind saying that again so I can get it right?" It might take a few tries, but the other person always feels special, because I am making such an effort to get it right.

Or I ask them how they spell their name: "Is that Caroline with an *i* or a *y*?" Or I might try to connect their name to something else: "My grandmother's name was Julia. I've always loved that name."

One time, a guy with a sense of humor introduced himself with, "Hi, my name is Bob. One *o*." Sounds really corny, right? But I never forgot his name, and I always smile when I think of him.

Maybe when your guardians introduce you, they can say, "ZsaZsa. Like the movie star, only younger. You can also call her *Dah-ling*." What do you think?

Love,

Auntie Ness

Dear Auntie Ness,

Did you know that my guardians changed my name? I was originally ZsaZsa *GaPooch,* like Ms. Gabor, only poochier. Or that Lady Gaga, but with more ZsaZsa— *zip!* But my name was so hard for people to say that they changed it from "Ga" to "La." It may sound *tres parfait* for a French bulldog, but I was still upset.

When I was GaPooch, I thought I might be the next big classic film star, perhaps as Toulouse-Lautrec's dog in a remake of *Maulin' Rouge.* Who's going to offer me a screen test now with a name like ZsaZsa LaPooch? Perhaps I could help LaLa Gaga make a new music video. I hear that she is a Diva. I have heard some of her songs, and I believe she could use a background barker (me) to yip, or try to howl:

> *"Ruff-Ruff Arf-Arf-Aa-arf*
> *Rowf-Ah Rowf-Ah Rah-ah*
> *ZsaZsa Ooh La La..."*

Then again, maybe I should just stick to using my good looks. Maybe I could make a cameo appearance in an adult film as Fifi or, even better, Fido LaFlesh?

I hesitate to discuss that idea with Jim or Mary.

Love,

ZZ

Dear ZZ:

Since you retired as official amateur therapy dog when Jim closed his medical practice, it sounds like you are not content simply being Snuggler-in-Chief and Guardian of the Gate for Mary and Jim. If you are thinking about establishing a new career for yourself, we should talk. I may have some suggestions for you. But I do not think music videos or the adult film industry would be right for a pooch of your high breeding, the Mayflower Madam notwithstanding. Give me a few alternative ideas.

Love, and patient understanding,

Auntie Ness

16

Making the Most of Your Mojo

Dear Auntie Ness,

Have I ever told you how much I enjoy banks? So much that I have decided I would be very successful in the banking industry. Actually, I am already.

Every time I go into a bank, the staff admire me and give me treats. Don't you think that is a good start? But it doesn't stop there! All the people waiting in line smile. Of course, I give them loving looks and let them scratch my neck. Everybody likes that, including me. I've noticed that people are much friendlier when I am there. In fact, one bank has my picture on the wall. They say I am their mascot. Fortunately, it's a very flattering picture of me—otherwise, I'd object to being trivialized. I mean, how long will it take for everybody to notice that I'm really the boss of them?

But I know better than to leave a deposit. I only make withdrawals—I get treats. There is no banking crisis as long as there are treats. It is as simple as that.

Obviously I bring out the best in people, which is an important skill. Do you think I would be an excellent banker?

Love,

ZsaZsaLa

Dear ZZ:

It is admirable that you are thinking of a career. I am impressed you are trying to plan ahead, because you are one who is so much of the moment. I am glad you asked because, while I will never be of the moment, I do know a thing or two about planning ahead.

So, ZZ, let's get real. Let me offer you the following, my little cute one:

Guidelines for Getting Ahead in the Banking Business

- What degrees have you earned? Bachelor's? Master's? Is an MBA required? MBA does not stand for Master of (French) Bulldog Actions. What is your major? Or let me put it more directly, did you ever graduate from high school? Have you ever even heard of high school, much less college? By the way, a number of colleges use bulldogs as their mascots. Yet, to my knowledge, none of them has chosen a French bulldog. So the field is wide open, if you are interested.

- Do you like math? How well do you count? Do you understand the prime rate, the stock exchange, and treasury auctions? I know you understand the treat equation, which is very important. I also know that your emotional intelligence is high, as is your ability to be cute and connect with humans.

- Have you ever written an application for employment? Do you have an employment photo? Can you email your résumé to the HR department?
- Did you check out the job description? Is there a height limit? After all, you stand less than one foot high, and the people you'd be working with are probably five feet tall, or more. You may be challenged here. You have to look them in the eye, you know. That's a big part of the social interaction. But mind you, I do not recommend your entertaining a job discrimination lawsuit about this issue.
- Do you know any real bankers besides the treatgivers?
- Do you have an "in" at your local bank? Do you know the branch manager or someone who would look kindly on your employable skills? Try to learn the word *networking*.

I think, ZZeeeeeeeeeeeeees, and with all due love and licks, that, as with so many of the young generation just entering the work world, your approach is a bit ill-advised. Did your personal assistant let you read (by the way, do you know how to read?) that news article I sent to her? It talks about the new reality for misguidedly entitled Millennials? You, I think, are still in the old reality.

So, ZZZZZZZZZEEEEEEEEEEEEEEEEs, without killing your dream, or asking you to burn all of your pinstripe suits (whatever you do, please keep the pearls), let us readjust your employment sights. I don't think you would make a good banker, because you don't have the academic skills, the counting skills, or the demeanor.

This is no big deal, because not everybody can be the CCI (Chief Canine in Charge). Primarily because you don't have an MBA or even a CCC (Canine College Certificate), I think you should be a greeter, rather than a banker.

Walmart has greeters. No degree needed. We should look up the job description to see if your skills match. (Do you know what a job description is?) Lots of other places use greeters, and many give out treats.

As a greeter, there are some caveats for you, and these are big questions for a fun-loving gal like yourself. Do you think you would be able to do the following:

- Pass out treats and not keep them all for yourself?
- Answer questions and point people in the right direction?
- Scratch someone else's back without getting a scratch in return?
- Be okay as a blue-collar worker? (Yes, I know, your preferred color is pink, but we all must adjust to the new dress code reality.)

So, ZEEEEEEEEEEEEEEEEs, to answer your question: Yes, you could work at a bank, but not the way you envision it. You know, ZZ, we must all adjust our dreams as our lives take their licks. I know it is a hard thing to do. Even I have trouble with this one. (I, of course, will still love you no matter what you decide to do.) The important thing is that you're thinking about this.

Tails up!

Auntie Ness

Dear Ms. Forman:

   ZsaZsa will reply in her defense. However, she has requested that she have a couple of hours to compose herself, such is her level of irritation. She remembers quite clearly telling you that she had considerable experience as a greeter in Dr. Weber's office. She feels she is ready to move on to something equally productive during her limited waking hours.

Respectfully,

Mary M. Mitchell

Personal Assistant to ZsaZsa LaPooch

Dear Auntie Ness,

First, you're dogging me again with the tail wise-cracks? I am not only smart, but perfectly smart-looking with what Dr. Jim calls my "vestigial tail." But I am even more bummed that you don't think I can be a banking big shot. However, with all the talk now of politics' effect on financial markets, I am not sure that I want to participate anyhow.

This does not mean I don't give a lot of thought to my calling. I have many natural gifts, and I am always sniffing out opportunities for a good life, filled with love and lots of treats. Just yesterday another idea jumped into my mind.

Mary and I were out for our daily playtime. That's what she calls it. I call it watching my figure. We run and jump, and I bounce balls off my nose, then chase them. We always have two balls going at once because I get bored easily.

Anyway, a woman came out of a building that over-looks our grassy field and told Mary that she and her work team enjoy watching us play, because they never saw a French bulldog fetch before. (I bet she was also impressed I use two balls. That's because I'm no dork like Lassie. I'm not about to let one ball go unless I know I can get another right away.)

Regardless, she went on about how cute I am. Then she (finally) said something I didn't know already! She and her office pals really like seeing all the different sports bras I wear. *Sports bras!* Well, I never thought of my leash harnesses that way, but she is right.

So now I'm thinking that my career should be modeling bras. Mary says there used to be a famous ad that said, "I dreamed I was ... in my Maidenform bra." Think of the possibilities! There could be a whole campaign, starring me. I'll have the bra-wearing nation repeating my catchphrase:

I dreamed I was ZsaZsa in my [Lucky Sponsor's Name here] sports bra.

My figure is still trim and fit, which will appeal to sponsors. In fact, I think I need an agent. Please advise soon. I'm not getting any younger, you know, and there's no time to waste. Who wants to be a banker anyway?

Love,

ZsaZsaLa!

Auntie N! Auntie N!

I couldn't wait for your reply. I am now a cover girl and will be henceforth. To think, all this palaver about a vocation when, all the while, my true *métier* was staring me in the face every time I looked in a mirror.

I have landed the back cover of *Etc.,* the Seattle Pacific University magazine. Yours truly stars in a full-age color photo! I am wearing my green leash harness— I mean, sports bra—which perfectly complements the front lawn on which I am standing. The dramatic lighting in the background is vaguely reminiscent of a divine presence, which, not incidentally, shines on my much-praised *derriere.* The photo also shows my muscle tone and figure to full advantage.

The shot was taken when Mary and I were gamboling on the SPU lawn, as we often do. My expression is one of which you, as a Diva, would approve. The headline reads: "Don't Drop the Ball." As if I ever would, unless something better, like a treat, was proffered.

Where was my agent when I needed her? I haven't been awarded any treats for this photo shoot—not yet, anyway. Jim has started negotiations on my behalf. Which fitness company, do you think, would best appreciate my endorsement?

I wonder if I should get business cards. They could read:

ZsaZsa LaPooch
Motivational Model

Forget banking. Really.

L & L,

Zips

[The photo referred to above may be seen on back cover of this book with permission from the photographer, Luke Rutan.]

My darling (poor misguided) Zipette:

Truth be told, you do look captivating in this candid photo. I am so glad that your green sports bra and the grass match with the halo-effect doggess lighting. (This is very hard to do in a catch-as-catch-can photograph.) Obviously you were at the gym earlier in the day, because, as you say, you are buff and toned. What a joy!

Now, my little Millennial, let's get real. Yes, we have nixed banking as a vocation, and you have been retired as an amateur therapy dog, through no fault of your own. I can see where you might want something to fill some of the four hours you are awake each day.

However, as a cover girl or bra model, do you know what you would have to do? Have you talked to other models? Are you really ready to talk the talk and walk the walk? In your case it means dropping about five pounds to be stick thin. I don't think that meshes with the treat equation. Strutting your stuff on command before hooting and howling people and pooches—on a *cat*walk, no less?

I am not sure you are up for this kind of treatment. You are so of the moment that bouncing to someone else's ball is not your thing. Taking direction is something you have to work on. Not eating on demand … well … that is your biggest hurdle, oh mistress of treat-getting.

So, despite this superbly stylish photo of you, would you be willing to stand (or sit) for hours as the photographer perfected the lighting? Would you behave when you were asked to wear a furry sports bra in the heat of summer? You would have to, because the picture would run in the fall issues of fashion magazines. Would you be willing to forgo treats because you are watching your waistline? Would you be willing to smile on command? Oh, my little Diva-in-Training! Would you be willing to take the work conditions? Would you be okay not running in the grass after a stylist perfected your hair and makeup? I am afraid not.

ZZ, beauty is only fur deep. We have discussed this. You were lucky this time, because all the stars aligned in this one photo. Being a professional model (even a motivational one) is too much work and too stressful for someone of your nature. You must match your profession with your skill set, as well as your temperament.

It was a good shot, but get real. You don't need an agent. You already have licks and love from Jim, Mary, me, Peloton, and countless other people and pooches. And you are an experienced motivational amateur therapy dog, whose nature responds to treats and scratches.

Sorry to be such a downer, but a reality check is always important, especially for an of-the-moment poochette like you. By the way, if I thought your nature was better suited for it, I would have recommended that you embark on that bra-modeling career. (Perhaps *Maidenpaw*?)

Possibly in a different time, or if your nature changes. Still, keep dreaming and thinking about your next job. That is very important.

Love and Licks,

Auntie Ness

Dear AN,

You know, I almost had a real job recently. I don't know if it was intended as a paying gig, but I was asked to mentor Clover, a Portuguese Water Dog. Her guardians Janet and Steve invited me over for a tryout.

Imagine me, a role model for an impressionable pup! Or any kind of dog, for that matter! Can you just see the new canine trend: all manner of dogs dropping witticisms here and there, like so many pearls instead of, or alongside, poops? The possibilities for improved communication with humans boggle the mind.

Unfortunately, I overslept on what was supposed to be my first day at the job. And when Mary and Jim brought me over to meet my new charge, I was so cranky about being dragged away from a perfectly good nap that I did not put my best paw forward. In fact, I got so snarly that I even scared myself. I was so embarrassed. I am not inclined to try again with Clover. I say, let her fend for herself. She will grow up to be big enough to get by without my kind of attitude.

So, dear Auntie, I decided that I am not cut out to be a role model, or, if you are to be believed, any kind of model at all. Surely some other opportunity will present itself.

Sadly, yet hopefully,

ZZ

ZZ:

It was no accident that you overslept, then went on to bite yourself in the foot, so to speak. We have yet to come up with the right job for you. Are you really sure you even want a job? Why not content yourself with being warm, furry, and cuddlesome? What's wrong with that?

Look around. There is a lot of sadness in the world. You are pretty immune from many of life's problems, where you sit (or lie down). Think of all those starving dogs in Bangladesh. Thank Dog you live with Mary and Jim.

Fondly,

AN

Guess what, Auntie N?

Another opportunity presented itself. Do you remember my telling you that I got a birthday card from a new pup named Daisy? Well, I have been invited to her house to give her a few lessons in life. Unfortunately, she lives even farther away than you!

Jim and Mary have talked about taking me there on an airplane. They even bought this awful bag and for practice tried stuffing me into it. Well, you can imagine how I reacted: no way was I going to cooperate! Mary says it's the only way I can fly. I don't see birds flying all cooped up in bags. So why should I?

Daisy can fly out here if she is all that keen to meet me! So there's another gig I had to nix.

Love to you,

ZZ

ZsaZsa, my little Diva-to-be:

Under no circumstances should you allow anyone, even Mary or Jim, to stuff you into a bag. Divas cannot be properly admired while in bags. How would it be possible for others to admire your accessories, unless the bag was transparent, like a large Ziploc?

And kindly stop referring to mentoring opportunities as "gigs." Since time immemorial, Divas have regarded it as a duty and a privilege to attract and train potential successors. Just as I am teaching you, some day it will be your turn to teach others, lest the tradition of Divadom fade into obscurity.

As always,

Your Auntie Ness

Woofs to the Wise:

You must match your profession with
your skill set, as well as your temperament.

What Next?

Dear AN,

I am howling in protest right now, which disturbs what Dr. Jim calls my "homeostasis." Mary read a story online that some crazy hotel people in England are trying to put me out of a job! They are advertising "human bed warmers" service. They wear fleece suits and hairnets. They go to hotel rooms and get under the covers for five minutes to warm beds for perfect strangers!

This is not right! Some say that bed warming is what the French bulldog was bred for; other so-called dog breed experts say that it is *all* we are good for. They would be the same experts who would classify me as a "nonsporting" dog. Nonsporting, my hind paw!

Obviously, these breed "classifiers" have neither good breeding nor class. They have never seen me at the dog park. I play with the big dogs, and you know what? I herd them and keep them all in line.

And, as for these human bed warmers, I will neither sit nor stay still over this. I think of myself as professional and take pride in my work. I have honed bed warming to a high level of art. I guarantee you that I am more cuddlesome. Plus, I do not have to get out of bed when big people want to get in; I can stay all night. There is plenty of room for everybody, as far as I am concerned.

Your ZZ

Dear ZZ:

Do not be upset. Human bed warmers who wear hairnets? And leave the bed when the client arrives? That will not play in Peoria. It is a bad idea, and a terrible business model. It is unsanitary and has no class, taste, or style whatsoever.

ZZ, your current model will never go out of style. You give licks and love. What bed warmer with a hairnet will do that? Ugh!

Be of good cheer,

Your Ness

Woofs to the Wise:

There is plenty of room for everybody,
as far as I am concerned.

Dear AN,

Believe it or not, I just heard about something worse than human bed warmers. Now I am really throwing my paws up in disgust. Mary read online about something called Cuddle Parties. Apparently there have been thousands of them all over the world! And not one dog to show them how to do it right! Can you imagine?

Mary really needs to stop reading me things from the Internet.

What to do about this latest outrage? What if my natural talents in bed warming and cuddling are becoming obsolete?

I do have other talents, like herding big dogs at the dog park, breaking in puppies to fall in line—obviously behind me—protecting our home from intruders, making sure my guardians get enough exercise and rest. I could go on, but what's the use? If I list all my talents, don't you know some human will come along and find a way to cash in.

I think I need to lie down and think about something else. Perhaps I will have a cuddle day with Mary. Not a party ... just a day. Do you have a better idea?

Love and licks,

ZZ

Listen up, ZZ.

Cuddle parties? They are for losers. It is a marketing gimmick. Anyone in their right mind knows that ZsaZsa and friends are some of the best cuddlers around. Don't worry. It's just another ploy that will fail to unseat Man's (and Woman's) Best Friend.

However, here too is a lesson: Having a well-rounded life that keeps all of your talents and interests sharp is an essential Diva quality. Don't worry, Zeeeez. You will never become obsolete.

Cuddle days are very important. Very restorative. Very relaxing. A must! So rest assured. And when you awaken, go put on your pearls and bark with pride.

xxoo, and cuddle cuddle,

Your Ness

Dear Auntie Ness,

Some cuddle days are better than others. For instance, after two or three dog park days in a row, I am too pooped to plop, and all I want to do is spend the day in my private office under the bed. But the other day, while under there, I noticed bags were out and clothes all over the room.

Now when I see things moved about, I get really upset; I put my front paws up on Mary's or Jim's calves and hope they get the message that I need to be picked up and held. Frankly, I am afraid that somebody might be going away again. I tell you—it's a dog's life, Auntie Ness.

Love,

ZZ

Dear ZsaZsa:

Now that you are a young lady (well over twenty-one, I believe), it is time to get over the separation anxiety. As much as we love you, Zeeeeeeeeeeeees, everything is not always about you. Did you ever think Mary and Jim might need time of their own? Did you ever think that taking you to the park could be exhausting *for them,* especially if your guardians are not feeling up to snuff (or sniff)?

ZZ, keep up the bed warming and good cuddle work. That is important. Get over the *me.* Showing that you love your guardians is a must in any pooch's life. It gets you points, it gets you treats, and it gets you love. Be thankful for all that you have. Return that thanks with cuddles and kisses and licks and love.

xxoo,

Auntie Ness

18

Faux Paws and Apologies

Dear AN,

If I ever needed your advice, I need it right now.

Without beating around the bush, I pooped on my friend's floor.

I am in the doghouse. I fear I will be there forever now. And it is not a cozy place to be. I assure you that it was not my fault, but I cannot explain that to Mary or Jim, and certainly not to Bailey's guardians, George and Debbie.

Here is what happened. I was on the dock playing with Bailey, when Debbie stopped to chat with Mary. Then another neighbor joined them. Soon, we were all in Bailey's house, chatting and not paying attention to me. Mary forgot that the real reason we were out in the first place was for me to do my business and that I had gotten only half the job done.

While everybody was chatting, Mary became oblivious to my ever-pressing needs. I was frantic. I thought for a moment that I should slink off into a corner. But I decided that, no, I wanted somebody to see it and clean it right up. Most pooches would try to hide the evidence, but I am no sneak!

Well, everyone was horrified. Bailey's guardians won't let me in anymore, which means that I can't gobble up the cat food there. Mary and Jim are clearly embarrassed and not happy with me. If they only knew that I couldn't help it!

So, wise Diva, what do I do now to make it right? I really do not think I should have to live with this shame, do you? Shame is not good for my self-esteem, and it has caused the treat supply line to diminish considerably. Did you ever do something really embarrassing like that? What did you do about it? How did you get yourself out of the doghouse?

Love,

ZZ

ZsaZsaLa!

You what? You pooped on Bailey's floor? And you expect me to bail you out?

Are you crazy?

I will admit that there have been times when I have been at a really boring dinner party or a meeting, and thought something like poop on the floor just might relieve the boredom. But it only got as far as my imagination.

(You really must tell me if, in fact, the whole experience was somewhat liberating. But I digress.)

I admit that I have put my foot in my mouth many times and always, like you, with good intentions. By the way, did you put your paw in your mouth? Or were you too busy pointing it at other people, since you claim they are really to blame for the mess? That, Zeeez, is a major no-no.

Since you are somewhat challenged by the spoken language, I will outline for you how to give a proper apology. Probably, you lucky pooch, your guardians have done so already. The least required for an egregious error such as this is a handwritten letter and maybe even flowers.

A Guide for Getting Out of the Doghouse

- The most important thing to remember about making a faux paw is that nobody is perfect (Not

even me or you, my little Diva-in-Training), so we
need to keep a sense of humor about us. That goes
for how we respond to other people's foe paws too.

- The second most important thing is to apologize for
  any embarrassment you might have caused.
- Then—and this is most important—learn from
  your lesson. Never make the same mistake twice,
  and move on!

Shape up, girl,

Ness

Dear Auntie Ness,

I had not considered that I was pointing my paws at everyone else. There is something more I could have done. From now on, if I have to go, I will dig in with all four paws and make no bones about emphasizing my needs. No more socializing when I need to get down to business.

Yet I must ask you, dear AN, is it a faux paw to mark my turf? There is an older neighbor dog named Sonny here. Mary and Jim call him an "elder statesman," and he lets me push him around with nary a growl. His guardians had just bought him a new bed, and I felt obliged to mark it, if you know what I mean, so he would know that he only gets to use it with my permission, even if it is in his house.

It does not seem like a faux paw to me. It seems like a genetic imperative. I am sure you will agree, and I suspect that you have left your mark in quite a few places.

L & L,

ZZ

Now ZsaZsa,

I must ask you where you come up with big words like "genetic imperative." Sounds like you were listening to Dr. Jim again.

Regardless, I suspect I have made an impression here and there through the years. But there are other ways to do that, aside from evacuating your bladder. Why couldn't you have simply gone over and *sat* in the new bed, instead of squirting in it? If it were me, I would have given Sonny "The Look," and then dared him to move you. When he opted out, I would have simply tossed my head, left the bed and nonchalantly sauntered out the door.

That would have left quite an impression without leaving any stain (on the bed or on your character).

I suspect Sonny's place is another one where the door is no longer left open for you. Not that you have admitted as much to me. Am I right? Come on now, you can tell your Auntie Ness!

I still love you, although I think you need a few lessons in couth. Ask Mary for help. It is not too late. Never be afraid to make honest mistakes. It's how we learn.

AN

Cato

Woofs to the Wise:

Never be afraid to make
honest mistakes. It's how we learn.

19

What's an Operator?

Dear Auntie Ness,

I don't know what I would do without you to explain stuff to me.

The other day, my friend Missoula and Taylor, her guardian, took me to the dog park. I did what I usually do: ran, jumped, played, and bossed the big dogs around. I also stopped to nuzzle all the people who admired me. It was the least that I could do. Later, when Mary took me for a walk, I stopped in every bank we passed to get my pets, scratches, and treats.

After we got back from our walk, I nuzzled Mary as I always do. I like to turn my head so she can find that favorite spot on my neck. I never move when she is scratching me because I don't want to discourage her in any way.

Then, at the end of our scratchy-scratch session, she looked at me and said I am a "real operator."

What does that mean? Jim is a surgeon, so he must be an operator, but scalpels and my paws just don't work very well together.

Help!

Your not-so-little ZZ

My darling Zzeezala:

Let me explain. I think this relates to why you were so upset about those dreadful bed warmers and cuddle partiers.

Dear ZZ, it is *not* all about you. As cute as you are, you are not the center of most other people's worlds (except perhaps mine and Mary's and Jim's). You flit in and out of their lives each day. They are happy to greet you *in that moment*. Then, when you leave, they get on with their tasks, stresses, and family. You are merely a happy intrusion.

However, while the universe does not revolve around you, a Diva should always be the center of her *own* universe. (Keep this close to the ground, as only you can.)

Dearest ZeeZee-La, you so want to be adored, adorned, and treated that you put on this wonderful show to get people's attention. You push their "how cute is she?" button (you would be a great marketer), and they have no choice. They give you treats. That is your "M.O."—your *modus operandi*. And, yes, that makes you a not-so-modest operator.

Now, on to the more important stuff: If you can use your ability to "push people's buttons" for the good of others, then you have a great career path ahead of you. Let us discuss more, my little operator, button-pusher, treat-getter.

Remember that you should never belittle yourself for being so effective at what you do. It is an art, and I salute you. You should seek out job opportunities where you can be treated and scratched while doing good and making other people feel good about themselves, like being an amateur therapy dog. You have already done that. Now it is time for you to move on.

I suggest that you consider becoming a "reading dog." You need to find a mentor, perhaps Mary. You go to a school or classroom where kids have disabilities, whether caused by dyslexia, blindness, or other neurological problems. Perhaps they have an autism spectrum disorder. Or problems focusing and concentrating. These kids need extra encouragement to learn how to do something that is so difficult for them. Their disability makes them feel self-conscious. You know a little about that.

Consider the following:

A Reading Dog's Raisons D'être

- Mary can help you find a student and will tell him you need him to read to you. That way, the student gets much-needed practice by reading to a completely loving and nonjudgmental being— you!
- You can just sit there while Mary scratches, listening to stories old and new, and perhaps stories that can s-t-r-e-t-c-h your mind.

- If the kid stumbles, you do what you do best: look lovingly at the child, and Mary can prompt the kid to continue reading to you.
- If Mary asks the child, "Can you tell ZsaZsa what that word means?" then you can lick your chops and show your enjoyment, however you manage to do that without a tail.

Now ZZ, this is how you can change lives, get out of your self-centered, furry shell, and do good in the world, while getting treats, love, and licks in return. Remember: The more interests we have, the more alive we are.

Think about this kind of job opportunity; it is good for an upwardly mobile pooch like you. It can change your approach to life. It will transform your outlook from an opportunistic operator to one who is changing lives. That is an operator who is well worth her treats.

L and L,

AN

Woofs to the Wise:

The more interests we have,
the more alive we are.

Dearest Auntie Ness,

You make so much pooch sense. You are right. I do love being loved. It comes so easily to me. I also love other people, especially the ones who give me treats.

It is interesting that you told me to get out of my furry shell. Did you know that for years Jim has been telling people that I am a "little person in a fur suit"? But I digress.

For instance, when Mary was hurt and had a really bad "owie," I never left her side, and I know she felt better and recovered quickly because of me.

I am taking your words very seriously, because I believe I have gifts that can help other people. When Jim still had his surgical practice, I used to spend two afternoons a week at his office, just playing with the patients in the waiting room and making them happier. They were so scared sometimes.

Also, I used to go to the hospital and make rounds with him on weekends. It made me feel so good to visit the patients in their rooms. Sometimes they asked me to come onto their beds. Other times they just wanted to pet my head. And I should tell you that none of the patients ever gave me a single treat and, you know what? I never even thought about that until now.

This afternoon, Taylor told Mary and Jim that she is going to get Missoula certified as a therapy dog. I was excited because I've worked as an amateur therapy dog, and thought I would be the perfect pooch to teach her.

But Mary says that I have to earn a diploma to have credentials. So even though I already have experience, I have decided to become a *certified* therapy dog. Missoula and I will be students together, and Jim and Mary will help me with my homework. Taylor knows all about these things too.

We're going to a school called the Delta Society. When I graduate, I get to wear a special vest (I'll be soooo fashionable) and go to schools, hospitals, and nursing homes. I can help even more people than I already have. I won't expect treats from them, either. Wearing that vest and making people feel good will be my treat, I think.

Is this what it means to be an independent pooch? I think I am ready for higher education. You helped me see the light.

Love,

ZsaZsaLa

P.S.: I hope I get treats instead of that Master of Bulldog Action diploma you told me about.

P.P.S.: Do I teach you anything? I mean, you teach me so much. I really hope there is a *quid paw quo* here.

ZZ:

You *are* an aspiring professional office pooch. We don't have anything like that here in Philadelphia. Maybe you can start a trend.

All of us could use a little loving when we go to the doctor's office. I know I do. Having a kindly pooch there to greet and allow nervous patients to scratch her can make the nearly intolerable wait to see the doctor more manageable. It kind of softens the patients up so they won't be snarly when they finally get beyond the waiting room.

You know about snarls, don't you? Not that you ever have to resort to such unmannerly behavior. You know that one snarl begets another in response. And then where are we? Everyone starts snarling at each other. How can anyone expect to get any work done with behavior like that?

Of course, bottling up the snarls inside isn't healthy either. Maybe the best thing to do is to go into the bathroom or doghouse and get it out of your system there. Then come back all smiles. How do you show smiles? You don't have enough of a tail to wag to show happiness. Let me know about this. I really am curious.

And speaking of higher education, what have you taught me, ZsaZsa? Excellent question. Well, to begin, I've always been of the mindset that at work, one should be having fun at least 75 percent of the time. If you don't love it, forget it. It is too much stress.

But you have made me think about extending that to play time. You reinforced the idea that one should always find time or, rather, make time for play. Playing is good. Whether it be a fun run, dinner with friends, a walk in the park or down a city street, a movie, a play, reading a good (or even trashy) book, you should always take time to play, play, play: to run after the stick, catch a ball, romp in the grass, jump for a Frisbee, give licks and love, and get licks and love in return.

These are great stress relievers; they make me happy, they are fun, and they give me a new perspective in life.

I don't know what the ZZ equivalent to laughter would be, but laughing is also good. Laughing lightens the load and puts everything into a clearer picture. Laughter gets rid of pent-up tension, anger, frustration—all the bad stuff.

So, that is what you, my little ZZ-La, have taught me. Find time to play, laugh, love, and give licks. If need be, schedule it into your life every day. It's all good. Take that walk. Catch that ball. Giggle, giggle, giggle. Life is better after a giggle.

LL,

Auntie Ness

Woofs to the Wise:

One should always find time
or, rather, make time for play.

Dear Ness,

Funny you should ask me this. Here is how I live with my stubby tail disability and show happiness: I keep a kind of permanent grin on my face, especially when I am panting. I show happiness with my eyes and ears. Sometimes I cock my head a certain way. Jim and Mary know when I am happy.

They also know when I am not amused. I look off to one side and hold the pose to make sure they get the message. Absolutely no eye contact, even if they talk to me and try to cajole me into relenting.

But I rarely, if ever, snarl, except when playing tug-of-war. I never let go. I am a bulldog. You can play with me, but do not mess with me.

That is not bad office manners, is it?

Licks to you,

ZZ

Dear Little ZZs:

No, not at all. But be clear about how you feel. Consider the other person's feelings. I am sure you consider how Peloton feels before you bite him. I am sure you know the consequences of biting: he who bites last, bites best. You would never bite in anger, would you? You are much better trained than that.

Now a biting wit is something else again. I can teach you all about that, if you want to learn.

Smilingly,

Your Ness

Get Along, Little Doggie

20

Patience and Bedside Manners

Dear ZZ:

I believe that we learn from everybody, including dogs, so I am turning the tables. I need your take on this very important question, because you are an experienced therapy dog. So drop the ball. Turn away all treats of the moment. Sit down. Eyes ahead. And listen, listen, listen.

Sometimes I am so disappointed in people. It is when I am at my most vulnerable. What is vulnerable? It is when you hurt inside so much that you are susceptible to being treated badly. To put it another way, it is about our need to be treated right by difficult people who just don't get it.

It can happen in a department store or at the supermarket when checking out. It can happen at work. It can happen in a doctor's office. It can happen with phone or cable service providers—or lack thereof.

So, ZZ, I must tell you that I learned the other day that I have a health problem that will require very powerful medicine. I am scared. I know I will experience loathsome side effects and that I will lose my hair. To me, it is an outward manifestation of all that is wrong inside my body. I am very vulnerable and must admit I find myself weeping at odd times.

And, of course, my doctor, though brilliant (and I am fortunate to be in his hands), focuses mainly on gathering data, analyzing it, and treating the disease. He can't help it. He's hard-wired that way. That is excellent because that is his role. My role as a patient is to rely on his expertise, so I can make wise decisions about my healthcare.

And, it must be said, I do know that he is kind. He listens and has my medical interests as Number One on his hit parade.

But he lacks a comforting bedside manner, which I desperately need, dear ZZ. Even though I am surrounded here in Philadelphia and around the country by great friends, like Mary and Jim, I live by myself. I am angry and vulnerable and need more than just brilliance. Surely, dear ZZ, there is more to healing than brilliance?

I have decided to make it my goal to make the poor man see the light. Perhaps that will amuse me, give me some focus, and help me cope. Here is an example of what I mean.

My hair needed to be shaped, because it was not looking its best. I also wanted to color it one more time. So I emailed to ask whether having my hair colored would hasten its loss. His response made me very angry.

He replied that he didn't think coloring my hair would hurt. But he thought it would be, to use his words, "a waste of money."

That sounded like fighting words to me. Since I am a highly evolved Diva, time and effort lavished upon my appearance could never be considered a "waste of money." So I went to the salon and made myself look as fabulous as I could possibly be. Then I emailed to let him know that I *did* get my hair done. It was *not* a waste of money, because it made me feel good.

And, Diva that I am, I added that the next time he was asked such a question, he ought to think about the bigger picture—what his patients are feeling, not what is "practical." And certainly, not about money. Sometimes, when you are vulnerable, "wasting" money is the most practical thing you can do. Even if it only made me feel and look good for one day, it was worth it.

Then I closed by telling him that he seems like the type who would buy the woman in his life a practical gift, like a microwave oven, instead of a more thoughtful gift, like nice jewelry. I strongly urged him, in no uncertain terms, to get his brain out of the appliance aisle and over to the jewelry counter and be more thoughtful with his patients in the future.

I guess I was naughty, but I now have a goal: to transform bad bedside manners, one doctor at a time. Do you think this can be done?

L & L,

AN

Dear Auntie Ness,

I am surprised. It is very rare for you to ask advice of me, since you are so wise and experienced. Yet I do think that I can help you here. I have had to work with some pretty sad people in Jim's office. Some had to deal with serious sickness, like you. Others had different types of health problems, most surgically related.

I've also had my own health problems, like when I had that bad fall at the beach. And Mary or Jim told you Peloton had cancer, right? But his hair is short, like mine. He's never had to worry about questions of styling. He worries more about when his next meal is coming.

I am horrified to think your doctor is the type who might give his wife a microwave to wear instead of a necklace. You were right to be offended, and you have a moral imperative to go over to his office and explain the value of looking good. This man probably never gives a thought to things like the importance of a good hair day, just like Peloton.

Try to remember, too, that your doctor is well-intentioned. His wife probably loves him, even if he is the clueless type who gives her appliances instead of jewelry.

Also, I remember you taught me this: I always get into trouble when I expect Peloton to react the way I want. He is goofy, but I love him anyway, just the way he is. You don't have to love your goofy doctor. But you can accept that your doctor is there to advise you in practical health matters, not personal hair matters. That's what you have me for!

Get a grip, Auntie Ness! And get a mani-pedi, too, while you're at it. I just had my nails painted red. Really. It's all about the look, which I learned from you, even if the look only lasts a few days.

Speaking of my look (I know we really weren't talking about that, but we are now) I am concerned that my forehead is so wrinkly. I am thinking that I need Canine Cream. Or Dogtox injections. The problem is that I worry a lot. That may surprise you, but it's true.

Just the other day, I was in Mary's lap watching the news. To hear the TV people tell it, the world is a horrible place. I worry there is not enough peace in the world. Perhaps I should run the world. I know how to keep all the big dogs in line. People are just too quick to yap, "Cry havoc! And let loose the dogs of war."

I worry about you too. If you would like to come out here, I could sit on your lap and give you kisses and cuddles until you are well again. You know, AN, I am always here for you. Love is what I am all about.

L & L,

Zibbets Zee

Dearest ZZ:

Well, I am glad you shared with me about Peloton and his health challenges, as well as your own. It is so great that you are his best friend and give him love and licks, and help him find his next meal. I wish you were here with me in Philadelphia to help me through my sickness; I could use some of your special love right about now. I am not feeling strong enough to come out to your home in Seattle.

Now, ZZ, I must digress: world peace? Canine Creams? Now it's your turn to get a grip. World peace is a good goal, but I think you have a secret desire to be Miss America. You must know about this contest, because you are so pretty. (And do not dare ever get injections for those adorable wrinkles of yours. They are very becoming, and well-earned.) They always ask contestants about how they want to change the world. And their answer is always the same: "World Peace."

Going for a pageant sash and a tiara and being a Diva-in-Training are two distinct paths in life. Personally, I don't think they are compatible. Although some claim these pageants are about scholarship, talent, and beauty, we all know it is *really* about looking good in that swimsuit. (Do you have a swimsuit? Is it a bikini? What color is it?)

On the other hand—pardon me, on the other paw— being a Diva is about achieving the highest possible self-esteem in the whole wide world (with or without world peace). That's because the talent, scholarship, and a beach-ready body are a given. In fact, if there were more Divas in the world, you can bet there would be much more peace in the world.

You raise an interesting question: How does one wear a microwave? We must ponder it a bit. If on-the-go and wearing the microwave, where would you plug it in? Perhaps it would be better to wear a DVD. A circular saw, maybe. I got it—a lawnmower!

Love and Licks,

Auntie Ness

P.S.: Zibbets Zee? That is a new one on me. Where did that come from? Did you know I have a teeny tiny cousin who is only nine months old? His father calls him The Zibbit. The Zibbit is the cutest, most wonderful baby in the whole wide world. (Don't be jealous.) His nickname sounds so much like yours, though spelled differently. Spelling does count from time to time. Perhaps this is the clue we need to discover if we do indeed share that pedigree.

Dear AN:

I don't think I know how to get to Philadelphia. I only know how to get around my own neighborhood!

Jim started calling me Zibbets Zee some time ago. I guess I forgot to tell you. He is always messing with my name. But it really doesn't matter what he calls me— even Zippets, Z, or Small Sad Sam—I always know when he is talking to me.

Sometimes I answer him with any of a variety of sounds, which he pretends to understand. Once in a while I come when he calls. It depends on whether or not I think it is worth my time. I certainly won't come running if I suspect his plan is to put me in the shower. I generally try my best to avoid those.

In fact, there is only one time I have ever stepped into a shower stall willingly. I was doing one of my special lickety-split ball grabs with a somersault flip. But on this day I landed kerplunk, right into a mud puddle. You could hardly tell I was a mostly white pooch until I got a good scrubbing.

By the way, I do not have a swimsuit, although I do have a life jacket. I've only worn this ridiculous contraption twice. You saw me in it that time we went boating with Janet and Steve. Remember? I could hardly move. Another time, Jim and Wayne put it on me and actually threw me into the lake! They said something about wanting to see if it works. Well it did, but I don't need it because I can swim perfectly well. I just choose not to do so.

Since I do not have a swimsuit, I suppose that means I cannot enter a beauty contest to promote world peace. I will have to confine my Diva apprenticeship to my own little piece of the world.

L & L,

ZZ

My Little ZZ:

You really need to change your attitude about showers. You should be grateful that Jim is willing to share his hot water with you. A Diva simply cannot walk about splattered with mud. A Diva must always be ready to be appreciated at her very best. A clean body always makes a good impression.

Forever,

Your Auntie N

Woofs to the Wise:

A clean body always
makes a good impression.

21

A Better Way to Bark

Oh, Auntie Ness!

I was so upset today that I couldn't even eat my breakfast. (Actually, I always prefer to start with a bite or three of human food, as a sort of *amuse-bouche*—not *biche,* you understand—before polishing off what's in my bowl.)

But today is another story entirely. Today I am too upset to eat anything. And no treats either. Not until I get this off my chest.

Mary, Jim, and I (between naps) have been watching the TV, and I am so concerned about the crazy people out there who shoot other people. Why would a human try to kill another human? Certainly not for food; there seems to be plenty of food and treats out there for everybody.

Why can't they just learn to bark at each other, then walk away and forget the whole thing? Or maybe bite a few ankles to emphasize their point? (Hopefully without inflicting pain, the way Peloton and I do it.) What would be wrong with that?

Maybe I should be a Special Advisor to the American people. Now that would be the kind of job I might like, so long as I could still get in plenty of naps.

ZsaZsa LaPooch: Advice for Treats.

I like the sound of it. Will that, as you have said, "play in Peoria," wherever that is?

L & L,

ZZ

Dear ZZ:

Clearly you need more than your usual allotment of love and licks today. We all do. News of senseless killings is always disheartening. Humans are supposed to be the most highly developed beings on the planet, yet too often we behave as though we were no better—indeed, in some ways worse—than cavemen.

And it doesn't just happen in our country. Whether it is the shootings in Tucson or a suicide bombing half a world away, this kind of behavior is akin to you and your dog park friends acting like a wild pack of wolves. When you and Peloton playfully nip and bite each other, that is acceptable, civilized fun among friends. But when the biting is done with a snarl, with the intent to cause injury, or without any regard for the well-being of others … well, it may not directly cause a tragedy, but it almost always contributes to one.

President Obama reminded us after the Tucson shooting that "we may not be able to stop all the evil of the world, but I know how we treat each other is entirely up to us." As a Special Advisor to the American people, could you improve upon President Obama's exhortations for restoration of civility? Can you show humans how to disagree without being disagreeable? How to bark without biting, and bite without causing pain? When faced with a possible fight, do you take the time to sleep on it first?

Why do people kill? Why can't they argue, perhaps even fight, and then simply walk away? Because you are so mannerly and mellow, I know this must be confusing, and you are very wise to ask these questions. Asking questions, in fact, is the first step toward civility.

That's why it is essential, for people and pooches, to learn the skills for effective disagreement: how to pause (paws?) before barking. I offer them here, not because I have mastered them yet, but because, as the saying goes, "We teach what we want to learn."

How to Pause (not Paws) and Bark with Civility

Pause to ask yourself …
- Is the timing right?
- Am I in the right place to show my anger and raise up my hackles?
- Is this really worth going to the mat?
- What might happen if I lose this fight?

Bark …
- In private, if possible.
- With controlled emotions.
- Without a judgmental tone or accusatory statements. (For example, say, "I may not have been clear." Don't say, "You don't get it.")
- Without getting personal. No biting. Be respectful.

- On topic. Keep the discussion about the facts of the current conflict. Don't bring other issues into your discussion.
- With the big picture in mind, don't get caught up in who is right, or who is to blame. Focus on what needs to be done, what problem needs to be solved, and how to move forward in a way that's best for everyone.
- Then stop barking. After you have stated your case, be quiet and listen. Don't interrupt. Ask questions if something is unclear to you.
- Acknowledge and repeat back what you just heard. Be willing to change your own mind.

You wrote that you are concerned about world peace. You are already much more than a Special Advisor. You are the High Ambassadress of Love and Licks. You could be an American heroine. We need more heroes (even if you have to nap from time to time).

So go for it, kiddo. My money is on you.

xxoo,

Auntie Ness

P.S.: "Will it play in Peoria?" means if it works in the heartland, it will fly anywhere.

22

People Can Be Biting Too

Dear Auntie Ness,

I am so upset. Tonight I went to an art exhibit opening with Jim and Mary. I got dressed up in my best pearls and was very happy to be there. The artist is a friend, named Perri, who sometimes stays with me when Jim and Mary are away. She has won Fulbright Fellowships; plus she is very loving, and we all think she is wonderful.

Well, I was admiring one of Perri's works of art when a woman pointed to me and said, "Look how ugly that dog is!"

I looked around to see what slouchy, nasty-looking dog she was referring to, only to realize that it was me. I was speechless. It made me feel just awful. If I had a tail, I surely would have put it between my legs and cried.

How can people be so cruel?

Mary said not to take it personally because that woman is a scientist and not from this country. I know

Mary was only trying to make me feel better. She was hurt; Jim too.

I hope I can sleep tonight.

Sadly,

ZZ

My Dear ZZ:

First thing is, pick up your head. Stand tall (relatively). Check your lipstick and mascara. Reapply if necessary. Readjust your pearls. Find your true love, Peloton, and go to Norm's for a snort and get some licks and love on the way. You need it now.

How dare anyone insult my ZZ?

A scientist you say? Huh! I am outraged. Perhaps all the data points from her last failed experiment are swirling in her head. The bottom line is that there is no excuse for rude, nasty behavior. Being smart doesn't mean that you have people skills. She ought to be sent back to school for a remedial course in human relations. She has none.

A person never insults another person by saying something unpleasant about their looks. (In my book, Zzeeeeeeeeeeees, you are cute, adorable, and beautiful.) That was bad, bad behavior. Time out!

Can we excuse her? No. Rude is rude. Can we make excuses for her? No. Not even if she comes from someplace like Australia, a continent first settled by convicts, murderers, and felons. Did she smell like a marsupial? Oh so naughty on my part. Perhaps she looked like one and was jealous of your natural beauty.

Was what I said just now rude? No, because I didn't say this out loud or direct it to a person whose clothes and hairstyle may need of attention because of a personal crisis. I know something about this.

This insulter has no style. She could use your help in that department.

Instead of being swept into her nasty whirlwind, let's talk about what your response could have been. Remember our Diva lessons: A Diva never gets involved in other people's misery because it takes a toll on our temperament and looks.

When she first stepped into your realm and said those nasty words, you could have snorfled pleasingly and used all the cuteness you could muster to make eye contact, as if to say, "Excuse me, what did you say? Was that directed at me?"

Then, after you were sure you had her attention, you could have ignored her. Walked away. Taken the high road. She was not worthy of any more of your time. No heated discussion about esthetics with someone so crude. A Diva never gets sucked into that. You are above stepping into others' nasty auras. Move on, save your energy for Peloton, playing with Mary and Jim, and writing to me.

For future reference, the question is, what defines beauty? First let me say that, after years and years of looking at art, I have many thoughts on this matter.

Beauty, as the cliché goes, is always in the eye of the beholder. What is beautiful to one culture or person may not stand the test of time for another. Every generation rejects the idea of what turned on their fathers and mothers and finds their own sense of beauty.

Look at music, from ballads to rock to hard rock. (I am proud to say, I fell off the rock-and-roll plateau in the late 1970s.) Look at ancient cultures, like the Egyptians, BC (Before Canines). They thought a beautiful woman had an elongated neck, outrageous cat eyes and long, slender fingers. The Greeks idealized the human body to a self-image without blemish. People from those two cultures would not have understood the art of the other.

Did these cultures produce ugly art works? No, not ugly. The answer is *different.* When we look at a painting (besides taking in the colors, the composition, and the theme), we must think about why we don't respond to this, why our hearts don't skip a beat the way they do when we see something beautiful.

The answer is this: different standards, different ideas and ideals, different times. *Ugly* is not a good word to use. It is pejorative and mean. We learned in Diva training never to be mean.

So, my dear Zeeeees, get a move on. Ignore the rude people of the world because they are not worth our attention. Focus on beauty, and you will find it. Go play with your true love. This is another way to make your heart skip a beat.

Much love and licks,

Auntie Ness

Dear Auntie Ness,

Sometimes I can't believe how mean people can be. Just today, a man walked by me on the street and said I have ears like a bat. Can you believe that? I ask you, is that any way to talk about a personal GPS system as effective as mine?

But that wasn't the end of it. Two ladies walking past then started making smoochie sounds to me and asked if they could give me a scratch. Mary obliged. Well, in the middle of the scratch, one of them cooed, "She is so sweet. She looks just like a little pig!"

Imagine how you would feel being called a bat and a pig all in the same innocent walk around the block! But Mary said that she was very proud of the way I handled it: I was simply too polite to notice they were being so nasty. I was following your advice in taking the high road, which is not as easy as you might think, considering how low to the ground I am.

What do you think I should have done? Should I have pinned back my ears and growled? Should Mary have told them off?

Love,

ZsaZsaLa

Dear ZZ, Diva-in-Training:

A bat? Cute as a pig?

We would have to understand where these folks are coming from to understand why they would say such things. What happened to them this morning? Maybe someone suggested they were having a bad hair day. We would need to figure out what, if anything, was going on in their heads. But, alas, that is the role of a shrink.

Yes, Mary could have told them off. Perhaps with a subtle, "Are you lost? Don't you know your left from your right?" But you, ZZ, stood tall, relatively speaking. Why engage in nasties when you will never see these mean or misdirected folks again? Be your sweet self. If you get sucked up into their whirlwind, you will be miserable all day. That is not what you are about. You are about barking and treats and giving licks and love.

Now, if this persists, and you get the oinker moniker again, Mary can simply tell the offender: "I know you mean well by calling her a pig. However, where ZsaZsa comes from, that is an insult. ZsaZsa would appreciate it if you would please tell her she is a gorgeous doll instead." That would make you perk up and wag your tail, if only you had one.

Mary could also say, "ZsaZsa has bed bugs. Ergo, please don't scratch." Even better, she could return the favor and scratch them back.

As for the GPS-er, have Mary tell him: "That hurts ZsaZsa's feelings. She can't help it if she has a perfect sense of direction. She was born with that gift naturally. We are proud of her."

If I were feeling better, I would pop right on a plane and come out to tell these rude people a thing or two. I would get right in their faces, the way we do here in Philly.

Love and licks,

Your Ness

Dear AN:

I am glad that you get into people's faces too. The closer I get, the better I can sniff!

ZZ

23

Clear Communicating, Before It's Too Late

Dear AN,

I don't mean to bark at you, but I haven't heard from you for a really long time. I am worried. Aren't you better yet? Or am I barking up the wrong tree?

Barking, by the way, is not something a smart pooch does frequently. The barks would lose their dramatic impact. I have different barks for different occasions.

Squirrels: This is the most energy-intensive of my repertoire because, you know, they're squirrels! I bark just short of the point of hysteria until they find another tree to hang upside down from.

Raccoons: This bark is slightly throatier than my bark for squirrels. I pair it with low, deep growls, which Sonny, my silly old pug neighbor on the dock, probably finds sexy.

"I Can't Reach My Ball": This one is somewhat pleading, with a plaintive, helpless tone. When my call for help is answered, it is important that I look up with an adoring smile.

"You Are Trespassing": This is a brief, intense, and menacing little bark, but without any ferocity. It's a challenging balance.

I do have other ways I communicate too. Nonbarking communication is my specialty. With my negligible tail, I've had to be more resourceful in how I show happiness. But with my big eyes and expressive ears, I always seem to get my point across.

Peloton likes to howl, for reasons that are not apparent. I've tried this only once, but it didn't suit me at the time. I'll work on it some more, if Lady Gaga lets me audition as a Spot in one of her videos.

Please write soon. I miss hearing from you.

L & L,

Your ZZ

Dear Auntie Ness,

I am so upset. The other day, I lost two tennis balls in the water, and I couldn't climb over the rocks to get them back. Mary was extra-specially nice to me afterward. She told me that she understood I was sad, and later—can you believe it?—she bought me some brand new balls.

That was very nice of her, but they weren't the same. My old tennis balls had a special taste that I liked. They bounced perfectly. Not too high, not too low. These new balls are good, but they are not the same.

It is strange. I have new balls, but I still feel sad that I do not have my old balls any more. In fact, I do not think I can write any more about it. Remembering makes me too upset. I will be leaving to play with Peloton soon. Perhaps that will cheer me up.

Your Zees

Dear Sad ZZ:

Sometimes I get too upset to talk about things—for instance, my own health problems. People keep calling to find out how I am, and I really don't want to talk about that. I continue to be ill, and I would rather talk about healthy things and focus all my energy in that direction. So thank you, Zees. Your questions and need to know have again made my day.

Now, let's get on to the important stuff. I bet those balls mean a lot more to you now that you have lost them. Maybe you even wish that you had taken better care of them. You prized them because they made you happy. When you played with them, they might have brought out the best in you. So losing them means you are losing a part of yourself, and that feels sad. It hurts, especially because you can't get that part of yourself back.

But here is the important thing, my little Zees. When the old balls are gone, this is also an opportunity. You can play with new toys. Perhaps instead of new balls, you could try playing with a favorite stick. Or a new Frisbee. What fun! I bet you never considered that possibility.

The point, ZZ, is that it is painful to lose something you love. It hurts. It can be scary. I have given this much thought, and I have decided that the thing you love may be gone but—be it a ball or a friend—as long as you keep good memories and appreciation of what is gone, it is always with you, even as you learn to enjoy that new toy.

It will never be the same. It shouldn't be. But that is okay, because in some ways, it will be made better through all that you learned and loved of your favorite old toy.

Be sad, dearest ZsaZsa. But also be happy, because now you have a chance to find happiness in new ways, with your new balls.

Your Ness

Auntie Ness,

I wrote to you to feel better, but now I am so upset, I cannot even eat. That hardly ever happens. How can you say that a friend can be replaced like a ball? Don't you know how scared I was when Peloton had cancer?

It was a while ago. Peloton being sick is not even what was so scary. It was the way everyone acted. One day he was fine. The next thing I knew, he was gone. He was off-limits to me for several days, and, when I finally was allowed to visit, I wasn't allowed to give even one small bite on the ankle. Jim carried me over for a quick sniff. Peloton was kind of skinnier than usual, although he seemed happy enough to see me.

Mary and Jim talked about it with Peloton's guardians. Something about having his spleen removed. Do you know what that is? It sounded important. I don't know if he ever got it back. What scared me, though, was that everyone was afraid *he* wouldn't come back. I did not know what to do. I couldn't even think of my life without Peloton. After a while, he got better. Now he's back to his usual nonsense and is as weird as ever.

Something scary happened to Jim once too. That scared me so much I can't even talk about it now. Thank Dog he got better too. But I do not think I would ever want a new Peloton. Or a new Jim. I do not think that is even possible.

Auntie Ness, please write back soon. You have been taking so long to answer me. Explain to me how you think a friend is the same as a ball.

ZZ

ZEEEEEEZZZZ!

The last thing I intended was to upset you. Of course a friend is not the same as a ball. A friend is so much more, in so many ways. This is a most important matter. So sit up. Paws down and ears at attention. It is time to listen, listen, listen.

You know, Zeez, it's pretty much the same with Peloton and anybody you love. When we love somebody, they always seem to mean more if we lose them, or when we are afraid that we might lose them. Peloton survived a bad scare. You did too, because you cared for him. That means that you should love each other a little more, a little better, right now. I mean today.

Are you paying attention, Zeez? It means you should overlook how clueless he is sometimes. After all, maybe part of the reason you love him is that he is clueless. Maybe he loves you because you love him that way, just as he is.

Now, as for what a spleen is ... that is not important. (And you can ask Dr. Jim about that anyway.) The point, ZsaZsaLa, is that you should not focus on what Peloton is missing.

Focus instead on what is still there: Peloton's handsome demeanor, his white paws and collar, his annoying yet winsome howl. (After all, how many of us have males who sing to us?)

I have lost important people too, Zeez. My brother. My mother. Dear, dear friends. It really never stops hurting. I want to call or email them when something reminds me of them. Then I realize that they are not there anymore. At first it is very scary and feels very raw. Eventually I come to smile about the things I remember: the laughs, the not-so-funny stuff, and the things we did together. It makes me more determined to make every single moment matter. To be the best person I can be. That honors their memory, right?

Thank you for asking me this, ZZ. It is a very tough topic, and there are no easy answers.

Love,

AN

Dear Auntie N,

As always, you come up with such good advice. I do love Peloton, and, if he were any less goofy, I would probably not love him so much, especially because I get to be the boss of him, even when he gets to my food bowl before Mary or Jim can put it out of his reach. After all, there always seems to be plenty more food to refill the bowl after he is gone.

The important thing is that he keeps coming back. And I know that it's not just to see if there is any food lying around. You see, he loves me too.

And I love you, Auntie Ness! I know that you will get better soon, and that you will come back to see me.

Loves and Lots of Licks,

Your Zeez

P.S.: By the way, I made a decision the other day when Mary came in with some new tennis balls: I started hoarding them in my office under the bed where nobody but I can get to them. Even I have trouble reaching them. But this way, I know I have a stash, all safe and sound.

24

Grudges

Dear Auntie Ness,

I have an important question for you: What is a grudge? I ask because Mary says I am holding one.

I can hold chew bones and toys in my paws, but to the best of my knowledge, I have never held a grudge. You made a point earlier in my Diva-Ness training not to hold grudges.

Now I am confused. Should I hold one, if I can find one? Is a grudge a good thing? If I hold one, will that earn me a treat?

I must tell you that I definitely deserve some treats. Mary went away for days and days. She left me feeling blue and alone, except for Jim, and he is not very good at girl talk. And he was pretty blue himself.

There we were, the two of us, moping around the place. It was quite a sorry sight. It got to the point where Jim started eating his dinner with me—sitting on the floor. It has since become a nighttime ritual whenever Mary is gone.

Anyway, when Mary finally did come home, she kissed and hugged me and acted like nothing had happened. The nerve! She didn't even apologize for leaving me.

And here is the worst part: She *claims* that she went to visit you. I find that hard to believe because I am certain you would have written me about it.

Mary has been home for a week now, and I am still miffed. I can't even look at her. When she heads my way to play, I go off the other way. I even cuddle extra with Jim to punish her for leaving me. That's when she said I was holding a grudge.

Obviously, she is not a full-time guardian. Please tell me you are not a part-time Diva. You rarely write anymore. Thank Dog for good old Jim. He hardly ever goes anywhere for very long.

Love,

ZsaZsa

My Dear Little ZeeeeeZ:

This is one way in which we are alike: I too have never been one to be patient. But I am learning to be more of the moment, just as you are. I must ask you to be more patient with me. My illness keeps me from writing sometimes. I just need to get my priorities straight.

Don't fret about grudges. I will say this to you: do not hold grudges. They are unbecoming and weigh you down. The real question is this: Can one be both a Diva and a Babe?

xxoo,

Your AN

Dear AN,

Yes, absolutely. At least, I think I can be both a Diva and a Babe (though I am still only a Diva-in-Training).

I can also walk and chew gum at the same time. I have noticed that Divas do not especially admire Babes. Do Divas chew gum? I have noticed that a lot of Babes chew gum. But I have never seen a Diva do that.

What really matters is knowing *when* to act like a Diva and when to act like a Babe.

If grudges are that unbecoming, I will forget about them until I see one that I like enough to carry around. How does that sound?

Love,

ZsaZsala

ZZeees:

I think you may be on to something about the grudges, but not the gum. Nobody looks good chewing gum. Period. And I will do a better job getting right back to you.

Your AN

Woofs to the Wise:

Nobody looks good chewing gum.

25

More Bedside Manners

Dear ZZZZZZZZZZZZZZZZZs:

I need to ask you again about bedside manners. Sometimes, when I am not up to snuff (and that is more often lately), I see doctors. You call them veterinarians. Some of them are complete human beings and help me talk through more than just my medical issues. But some of them have no (that is *no*) bedside manner.

So, ZZ, please tell me how you work with your vets when they do not have a good bedside manner and do not pay attention to the total human (in your case, canine) being. So many of these doctors are mainly interested in data. That does not mean that they are not excellent at what they do. We would not be going to them otherwise; we just want something more.

How can we train them? Treats? Annoying emails that are also very witty? Or is it hopeless? Should we just stop demanding that they give more on the human scale than they may be capable of giving? I do believe that people can change and be helpful to others. You just have to hit the right buttons with them.

To tell the truth, I do better when I connect with the docs who are actually poking and prodding me. I am asking you, ZZ, because you have great expertise in this area.

xxoo,

YN

My Dear AN,

I am glad you asked me about bedside manners. When I used to accompany Jim to the hospital to get scratches, cuddles, and treats, I knew full well that my primary role was to help Jim make his patients feel better being in the hospital.

I could see that Jim had very good bedside manners. I never even saw him sit on the edge of a patient's bed. On the other hand, I was often invited to get up on the bed and snuggle. To the best of my knowledge, Jim was never invited to get into a hospital bed when there was a patient in it. I think that must be because he is such a big person, and these hospital beds are really only big enough for a big person and a svelte pooch like me.

After that time when Jim was taken away, he came home, but was in bed a lot. As soon as I was allowed, you can bet I was right there, back in bed with him. After all, we are family.

So, to me, good bedside manners is knowing when to get into bed with someone else, patient or otherwise, and when not to. Are you telling me that your doctors are confused about this? Do I need to write them a note and explain all this?

I love you, AN,

ZZ

Dear ZZ:

You are so cute, and you make me laugh, which is a good thing. I must tell you a story.

I was recently in a hospital bed, thoroughly sedated, as I should probably be all the time. My primary care physician came by at 9 a.m. to see what havoc my other docs had done to me. She sat on the bed, which I guess must have been a no-no, because all of a sudden, all kinds of alarms went off.

Who knew I was wired?

I can only guess the nurses were worried that I might try to escape the bed, flee the hospital, and get a good stiff drink. (Believe me, the thought had crossed my mind.) Why else would there be a secret no-no rule about doctors and bed sitting?

There was no Patients' Rule Book or Bill of Rights (and Wrongs) to guide me in this. There were no posted rules: "DOCTORS: KEEP OFF THE BED," or anything.

Most docs must have at least a modicum of etiquette ingrained in them to go along with their Hippocratic Oath: "First do no harm" (and, by logical extension, "Do not sit on the patient's bed—EVER"). Anyway, that got me thinking. I have noticed that when these docs do come to visit you, they always stand at the foot of the bed. I have often pondered why. Is it because they really are not allowed to sit on the bed? Does this give them a quicker exit strategy? Is it because it's easier to dispense good or bad information from a distance? Is it because it's easier to avoid eye contact that way?

I've seen you in action. You know something about giving and withholding eye contact. This is our opportunity to rewrite the rulebooks and give better guidance. Perhaps that is the best strategy. Perhaps they just need treats when they come to visit.

Now ZZ, there are other things we must discuss about bedside manners. I will send them to you, but later. I need a treat now. A nap. But I am right on top of this. I am so grateful that we can discuss everything, and giggle. I am thankful that you are always there for me.

I wonder, do Jim and Mary sit on your bed? I know you sit on theirs.

xxoo,

YN

Dear Auntie Ness,

I think you have it wrong. When doctors come into my room at the Greenlake Animal Hospital (where I was born), they bring me the treats. Why should I give them treats?

So for starters, I think that whenever anybody comes into your room in the hospital, they ought to bring you a treat. If you like your treat, then you can turn off the alarms and let them sit on your bed for a moment or two. In fact, perhaps they should keep dispensing treats to be allowed by you to stay longer.

See, you could have a timer by your bed, and a little bowl for them to drop the treats into, in case you don't feel like gobbling them up as soon as they are given. Do you see where I am going with this?

L & L,

Zips

My dearest ZZLa:

You know how much I love you. But people do bring me treats in the hospital. They bring candies, cookies, flowers, books. Anything they think will help me get better and cheer me up.

However, the docs and nurses do not bring treats. In human hospitals, maybe that's the sticking point! The docs bring news, information, and meds. They even have been known from time to time to take some of my treats, although it's more polite to wait until I make the offer. Admiring the flowers is okay. Sniffing them may not be. I think they should ask first.

I must say, though, that I have never seen a doctor look at the books I have on my bedside table. I wish they would do so. It would help them get to know me better—my likes and dislikes. They might even get some ideas for fun stuff to read, outside of science and medicine. Poor things. They need all the help they can get to lighten up a little.

Actually, ZZ, we humans can learn something from canine-loving, treat-giving hospitals. I think those treats in your animal hospitals are part of your meds regimen and your road to recovery. *Vive la différence!* Dear Frenchie, I will have more to say about bedside manners in a couple of hours. Right now I need a little nap. Stay tuned.

Oh, and Zzzzzzzzzzzzzzeeeeeeeeeeeeeeeeeeees, before I sleep, I must tell you that, in the human hospital, the people running the place control the alarms. We will have to work on that one, won't we? I think here you make an excellent point. Oh, it will be fun to be an alarm cracker (something like a safe cracker, but with more purpose).

Love and More Love,

AN

26

Training Over?

Dear Auntie Ness,

You would be so proud of me! Today I took a walk with Mary. (By the way, can you please get her to slow down and kick the leaves or smell the flowers more? She always legs it like she is on deadline.)

Anyway, we crossed paths with two people who, of course, stopped to admire me.

"She is really beautiful," said the woman.

"She is being a real Diva. She knows she is beautiful," Mary replied. (Mind you, I don't think she meant that in the most complimentary way, but I digress.) Now just wait to hear what happened next!

The man said, "Well then, she deserves to be a Diva!"

I could not wait to tell you! I have been recognized officially as a Diva!

Love,

ZZ

Dear ZsaZsaLa:

I am always proud of you, but at the moment you frustrate me. Let me straighten you out, dear little Diva-in-Training. You forget that, at first glance, all these people could do was comment on your appearance. Do not mistake me. You are inarguably beautiful. Just remember that you had nothing to do with that. Your good looks are a gift from your parents. It's in your genes.

You are not quite a Diva yet, but you are so very close if others are proclaiming you as such. They see your Diva-Ness emerging from within. You have just a little bit further to go in your journey to Divadom. You will not need to ask me. You will know when you have arrived.

I'll be there, waiting for you.

Your Ness

The Tail End

27

Dog's Honest Truth

Dear Auntie Ness,

   You never told me exactly why you are sick. You have been sick for so long now. I keep waiting for you to tell me. I guess it will take a few more weeks for you to get better. Should I sniff out how to come to your house, so I can give you licks and cuddles the way I used to do for Jim's patients? Then, when you get better, you could take me to meet Dr. Ben Franklin!

L & L,

ZZ

My Dearest Zibbets Zee:

I had hoped you would not ask me. I did not want you to know this, but a direct question deserves a direct answer. You know that I have been sick. I must tell you, my little Zibbets, that I have cancer. It is not the same type as Peloton's. The doctors did try to remove my cancer, the way they did with Peloton and his spleen. They couldn't remove mine, so they are giving me strong medicine to help me fight the progression instead.

This is why Mary has been disappearing from time to time. She has been coming out to Philadelphia to give me a hand. So don't give Mary the cold shoulder when she comes back—or me, for that matter, when I don't write you back promptly. She is my sister-of-choice, and I need her with me sometimes now. Give her licks and love; show her that you understand.

I worry that I will never get all better from this, but I intend to keep trying. I wish I had better news for you. But I can tell you that Dr. Ben Franklin would have liked to meet you. French females definitely mattered to him!

Love,

AN

Auntie Ness,

I am shaking. I have not been able to stop. It is hard for me to write. I have not felt this way since the time a long while ago when Jim got taken away. I guess I should tell you more about that now.

This one very bad day, Jim came home from teaching a yoga class and went to bed to lie down. Mary went in. Then she made a phone call. Soon, I heard all kinds of loud sirens wailing. Then strange men came to our door, but they didn't even look at me. They went straight for Jim.

They put him on a rolling table and put wires around him. Everything happened so fast; I could see something was very wrong, because absolutely no one paid any attention to me. Finally Mary picked me up.

That's when I started to shake and shake. I could not stop, no matter how hard I tried. All I could think of to do was run under the bed and stay there.

Then it got quiet. Nobody was around at all. I did not know what was going on. I thought I was going to be all alone forever; no one to feed me or take me outside to go potty. Or play with me, take me to the beach, or to Norm's for a snort. I can't even imagine how awful that would be.

Mary came back that night. She was upset, too, but Jim got all better and came home after a few days. But ever since then, I shake and run under my bed when I get scared, especially when I hear sirens or fireworks or fire alarms. Suitcases scare me too. That means Jim or Mary is going away.

I try my best to just ride it out. I stay quiet until I stop shaking. The only thing that makes it stop is to be held. Then I don't feel so scared.

I need to be held now. I will finish writing later ...

[Paws]

... I sat in Mary's lap for a while. She scratched me in all my favorite places. The shaking stopped.

Now I am angry.

I am angry with Jim and Mary, because they never tell me when they are leaving, or why. They also never told me why they took Jim away.

And I am angry with you, Auntie Ness.

Why would you not tell me you have cancer? You had so many chances to tell me. Do you think I am a dumb dog? I will tell you this: I think it was unfair of you to not tell me.

I am trying to put my paws in your shoes, because you told me I should not expect everyone to act the way I want them to act. Perhaps because you are so sick, it is too much bother for you to answer me. That is something I might understand. I am never one to give up my treats, but this one time, I will. I think it would be better for you to focus more on getting better now. Then we can finish my Diva-Ness training when you are well again.

So this time, please do not write back soon. Just wait and write back when you are better.

Forever your Diva-in-Training,

Zees

Oh, My Niecette-of-Choice:

What would I do without you to show me the error of my ways? You are mistaken about why I did not tell you sooner, but this time, dear ZsaZsaLa, it is I who was misguided.

You are my treat, Zees. I need you. I need your questions. I need you to tell me about your life in Seattle, going to Norm's, and playing with Peloton. I need your adventures at the dog park with the big dogs and your soccer games with Jim.

You see, Zees, this is the only chance I have to play anymore.

Here in Philadelphia, when I was well, I was quite the Diva about town. I know everyone, and they know me. I liked to walk—even when it's cold here, because no common cold ever touched me—on the streets of Olde City, the neighborhood where I live, near the Liberty Bell and Ben Franklin's house. When Mary lived here, we would see plays at the Walnut Street Theatre. I used to sip wine at the nearby Caribou Café, a French bistro (which you would like, were they to allow you in). North of City Hall on Broad Street is one of my favorite haunts, The Pennsylvania Academy of Fine Arts. I have spent countless hours there, especially since they acquired Thomas Eakins's *The Gross Clinic*. I have always coveted that painting.

Oh, the history this city I love holds for me doesn't compare one bit to the memories I hold.

Just a couple blocks west of PAFA is the Champs-Elysees of Philadelphia: The Benjamin Franklin Parkway, home to The Rodin Museum, The Free Library of Philadelphia, and another favorite hangout, the great Art Museum of Philadelphia. As we speak, they are even in the midst of building another art-lover's treasure on the Parkway, the new Barnes Foundation museum. How I wish I could walk through its halls on opening day.

How I wish I could go visit all my favorite places. How I wish I could show them to you. But you see, Zees, the medicine that is slowing my cancer is also making me quite ill. I cannot walk around my hometown anymore. I cannot even walk around my own home anymore. I am often in the hospital, confined to bed. I am too sick to enjoy a nice wine with my meal, if I can eat at all. I am often too weak to walk, or even sit up some days.

I am lucky to be surrounded by so many friends. I have wonderful doctors. (Some have questionable bedside manners, but still, I am grateful for them.) But it seems these days that the only thing my friends want to do is tell me to rest, or ask about how I'm feeling. "How's the treatment going? Have you heard about this new treatment? Have you tried this to help the side-effects?"

Everything in my life is about the cancer anymore. I am sick of it!

You, dear Zees, have been my treat and escape. Despite being ill, I have been trying to live my life as "normally" as possible. That means being the Diva that I am, within certain unavoidable limitations. Now the time for escaping is over. I need to get a grip and be as honest with you as you always have been with me.

I told myself that I did not want to worry you, but this time, my highly evolved senses did not serve me well. I suppose the real reason I did not tell you sooner is that ... well, that I am scared.

That is not an easy thing for me to admit. But I was recently reminded of my former colleague and friend at WHYY, Dr. Dan Gottlieb. He hosts a radio program that helps a lot of people deal with hard things, like feeling vulnerable and scared. He said, "If you want to bring dignity to someone's life, ask them for something."

I need you now, my Zees, my niecette-of-choice, to ask me your questions. Ask me anything, about my cancer, or anything else. Bring it on, Lady ZsaZsa. We are both barking with the big dogs now.

Always Your Auntie Ness

P.S.: You are, by far, one of the smartest pooches I have ever known, and in no way a dumb dog. You should not say such things about yourself, even in jest. It puts bad ideas about you in other people's heads. This is a digression, but also a lesson: What you say about yourself will always be heard by others.

28

Shake It Off

Dear Auntie Ness

When I was a puppy in puppy school, the instructor used to call me "ZsaZsa the Brave" because the big dogs never scared me. They really didn't.

I used to run and jump with them and get them all riled up. Then I'd gallop away as fast as my little legs would run and wriggle myself into a tiny spot where they never could fit. I have always been smarter than the big guys, even though I am small. Of course, whenever I did this, their guardians would laugh and talk about how adorable I was. That made me feel even more brave.

I do not feel brave now. I am shaking again. I did not even know it was possible to pretend to feel one thing but act like you feel another. You seem to do it so well.

Since you need my questions, please tell me, how do you not shake when you are scared?

Your Zees

Dearest ZsaZsaLa:

One of the things we have in common is that, while no one ever called me Nessa the Brave, I used to love to take on the big guys, outsmarting them at every turn. But now, every time I turn around, someone gives me bad news about my illness. This time, it seems like I can't outsmart them.

I do my best to pretend that I am okay and not really scared. I don't talk about it with my human friends, and I take every opportunity to change the subject. I never miss a chance to get into a test of brains and willpower with my doctors and their staff. I challenge my friends too. I guess I keep hoping that I will win. Deep down, I know that I won't.

I am shaking on the inside, especially lately.

But I have noticed Zees, that when I talk to you, I shake a little less. Maybe it is because you are a French bulldog, and not a bull-headed human.

So perhaps that is the next step for both of us, talking about it. This is where you surpass me. I have spent my whole life perfecting the human trick of feeling one thing, yet showing another. So for me, talking about it will take time. I am not so sure I can keep all of it bottled up any more, especially when I see so many people around who do love me and have more practice than I do in showing it.

That's why I admire you, Zeeeez, because you are able to talk about it. You are able to shake and look up at Mary with your big eyes and tell her to hold and cuddle you. I need to cuddle and snuggle, but I just can't. I always have been so good at telling others what I think. The problem here, ZZ, is that thinking and feeling are different. Maybe not for you, but surely for me.

That's why you have such a great gift to give, little one. When you give somebody love and licks, they automatically let you into how they are feeling. They play fetch with you, or they laugh, or they cry and cuddle you.

I wish you were here right now. I wish I could cuddle you right now.

Love,

Auntie Ness

Dear AN,

I am unsure about a whole lot of things. Like getting into water over my head. I can swim, but I really don't like to do it. When Jim showed up with that life jacket thing, I was okay, until he brought me down to the end of the dock.

Just before he threw me in—and really, what was up with that?—I thought that I had no idea what would happen. Whenever I feel that, I take the position that when nothing is sure, everything is possible. That didn't make me feel any better as I got tossed into the lake, but with all the possibilities in the world open before I hit the water, I had a feeling it would be okay. The life jacket did make swimming easier, but it didn't make it any less scary. So I think you know what I mean.

Let's both try not to be so scared. When we are, let's both not pretend to be braver than we really are.

We both need a good cuddle right about now, don't we?

I love you,

ZsaZsa

Woofs to the Wise:

When nothing is sure,
everything is possible.

29

Farewell to Dear Friends

Dearest Zee:

Mary came to visit me today. At the time, I was far too weak to talk or even open my eyes, but I knew she was there. She stroked my hair and whispered, "Ness, you are really beautiful, and I love you."

Well, it's good thing I couldn't talk just then. I would have shouted, "Get a grip! I believe in 'look good, feel good,' but right now I look awful! My hair is curly and white. (Who knew? It's been so long.) No mascara. No mani-pedi. And I am wearing this pathetic excuse for a nightgown!"

Now that I have some strength and have thought about it, I think I understand what she meant. Mary wasn't seeing a hospital bed wreck. She saw her friend, her favorite Diva (*c'est moi, bien sur*), and sister-of-choice.

As the Diva under my wing, Zeez, you must remember always to be more beautiful on the inside than out. Continue being the well-mannered dog that you are. Take lots of sniffs on those walks. Don't speed up. That will help anyone walking with you to appreciate those precious minutes they have. Do not growl or whine. Be happy to see people who love you, even when you don't know each other.

And for goodness sakes, be sure to pee and poop only in approved places.

Dear ZZ, you are wise beyond your years. There is much wisdom behind those ears! The heart-shaped spot on your back is not there by accident; it is there to remind everybody of what you are all about: being a little dog with a big heart.

I am proud to be your Aunt!

Snuggle a lot. I must rest now.

Love,

Auntie Ness

My dear, dear Auntie Ness,

Thank you for all the help you give me. I love you. You're the best auntie a dog could ever have! And thank you for acknowledging my manners.

It's really interesting that you should mention manners. Just yesterday, when Annie, my favorite walking buddy, brought me into the UPS store, Stephen, the manager, whom I love, said to all the big people on line that I am the best-mannered dog he has ever seen.

So, you see, I have learned a lot about petiquette and Divadom. It is gratifying that people can appreciate my high level of refinement in spite of my low level of height. And do you know what? I intend to try to keep a stiff upper lip, which is not easy for me, and to be proud in my bearing. I will always be grateful to you, Auntie Ness.

L & L,

ZsaZsa

A Note from Mary, Personal Assistant to ZsaZsa LaPooch:

I read the previous email to Nessa on the last day of her life. She squeezed my hand in acknowledgment.

Special Treats

30

ZsaZsa's Approved List of Suggestions for Collaborative Communication (spoken or whispered, but never before 8 a.m.)

Some might think one should speak to a dog in a commanding manner, but I will be doggoned if that will get you anywhere with me.

"Come." You've got to be kidding! Try enticing me. Offer a scratch or treat instead.

"Hurry, hurry." When crossing the street, but we all know speed is a relative thing.

"Look." Used to get my attention. This has gotten old and quite irritating.

"Not for ZsaZsa." You mean it might be for someone else and not for me? Are you kidding?

"Shower." I hide in my office under the bed, where you cannot reach me. Don't tell anyone this: if I'm not paying attention, you can pop me in for a quick douse. I actually like the toweling-off part and sit still when Jim does my ears, because they're among my best features.

"Nails." I might let you do this, but only if you promise to use a nail file instead of those ghastly clippers and give me some peanut butter when we are done.

"You're in charge." I do not like that. It means you're leaving me. So I will just not look at you and march right off to my office for a sulk.

"We'll be back soon." I have heard this before, and I just don't buy it.

"Let's go see Peloton." What took you so long?

"Let's go to the beach!" Don't worry; I know my way. If the first one doesn't look promising, I know where all the best beaches are.

"Go see Bailey." Only if there's nothing better to do, like sleep.

"Give me a kiss." Usually, I only accept kisses. But I will give you some as soon as you reappear after you left me "in charge" for a long time. By the way, if you're planning to leave town, no kisses for you. When I see the luggage in the room, I know very well what that means.

"Let me kiss your ears." I lean forward and present one ear, then the other.

"...your head." I can go along with this too.

"...your eyes." Once in a while.

"...your nose." Now that is going too far, don't you think?

"Want to go down to the end of the dock?" I insist on my evening stroll. Someone has to patrol the place to keep those pushy raccoons from taking over. Don't even get me started on the squirrels.

"You want to get up on the bed?" Need you ask? My fleece blanket, please. And don't forget to turn on the heated pad.

"Go eat your food/drink some water." Thank you, but no. I am French and prefer to dine late at night, when nobody is watching. I will be quietly sitting at your feet while you eat, just in case.

Woofs to the Wise:

Some might think one should speak to a dog
in a commanding manner, but I will be doggoned
if that will get you anywhere with me.

31

My Very Own Diary

2006

October 17: I am born, without much of a tail. I have four sibs: Tank, Elbow Dot, Runt, and I-forget-whom. My baby name is Head Dot. Can you believe it? I quickly become the boss of all of them. It takes an operation to get us all out!

November 7: Jim and Mary are introduced to me. I go right over to Mary and sit on her foot. I am already the boss of her.

November 10: My ears quit flopping over and stand up all by themselves, proud and perky.

December 12: I say goodbye to my sibs and parents and go home with Jim and Mary in a bag, with my head peeking out of the top. They stick me in a cage by the bed. Such foolishness. I hope they will get over it soon.

December 13: I meet Bailey, my first best friend. She thinks she's the boss of me. I am not used to that, but it's okay. I'll figure something out when I am bigger.

December 27: I go to the doctor's for a shot and a chip, in case I get lost. Not likely to happen. I always know where I am. They keep giving me treats. I might go back for more, but only if I must.

2007

January 14: I go to my first birthday party, for Charlie, and meet Peloton for the first time. We become the best buddies ever. Charlie is okay too. We dig a big hole in the dirt. Everyone says we shouldn't have done it. But the best artists are rebels. I intend to perfect the craft of hole digging when I grow up.

January 15: Puppy school. Everyone is so juvenile. They obviously just do not get it. This business of dropping everything and running to whoever calls you is not for me. I must humor them for now, just to show that I understand the game.

February 14: I love Jim and Mary; they are such easy marks. They let me up on the bed. Better than that, I've got them picking me up to put me on the bed. The cage thing is passé.

March 3: Done with puppy school. I am not sure if I passed. It doesn't matter; I can go up and down stairs now! There's practically no stopping me.

March 17: St. Patrick's Day. I have my first—and last—beer; it just doesn't do much for me. I snuggle under the covers now, every night.

March 27: I go to the hospital for a nap. When I wake up, my tummy is sore. I don't even know what happened. I hear somebody say something about no more puppies. Well, that's a relief. Who needs a smaller, cuter puppy upstaging me?

April 1: My tummy doesn't hurt any more. My godmother Oatley draws my portrait so I can have it made into my very own correspondence cards.

June 11: What a day. Jim and Mary take me to Gary and Faye's farm. I terrorize chickens, herd sheep, and get cornered by a pack of goats. Who keeps a pack of goats? I find a section of fence to skibble under for my getaway. Then I run around and roll in the grass until my coat turns green. Best time ever.

July 4: Scary day. There are these booming and shaking noises. And howling. And car alarms. I hope this never happens again.

August 9: Jim and Mary are upset with me, just because I jump out of Mary's arms and run across four lanes of heavy traffic. I have to. There is a flock of pigeons! Jim runs after me. Jim and Mary keep saying this is the worst thing I've ever done, and they nearly have heart failure. Not my best day. From now on, I will stick with chasing squirrels. Little furry fat faces.

September 1: Jim starts bringing me to the office with him to greet all the patients. He calls me an "amateur therapy dog," whatever that is. But if it means Mary sends us off with lunch and treats, then that's what I'll be. I get to play with people all day until I am one pooped pup.

October 17: We find out that I am welcome at Norm's, just in time for my first birthday party. Of course Peloton and Bailey are invited. All the other dogs who happen to be hanging around get a piece of my cake.

2008

January 25: Jim and Mary take me to a big hotel in Portland. Mary calls it the Monaco. The place is really cool! They give me special treats from their bakery, and I get to run up and down the hallways, chasing after tennis balls. I am as good as Charlie now with balls.

March 14: Jim and Mary forget to bring my toys with them when we drive down to Portland. So I make a long face, which isn't easy for a dog to do. Jim finds me a cool stuffed froggie (which I still have) for tug-of-war and of course a new ball. So everything works out okay.

June 1: I go to the dog park today. It is a play date with a whole pack of not-too-bright dogs: my best buddy Peloton and Charlie too. I go with smaller dogs twice a week, and go with big guys like Henry and Scooter once a week. That's fine with me; I round them up and keep them in one little area until they figure out *I'm* the one in charge. Then I let them go run their fool heads off, while I stay cool.

June 30: Jim closes his doctor's office. I do not get to be an amateur therapy dog any more. Bummer.

July 4: It happened again. All these lights in the sky. Horrible noises. A huge racket. The worst barking I ever heard. (Oh, that was coming from me!)

July 5: Jim buys me a soccer ball. I bat it to him with my nose, and he kick passes to me. I can keep the ball moving with my front paws while I run. Sometimes Mary confuses me by throwing two or three balls in different directions at the same time. I wish she wouldn't do that.

August 6: I have changed the rules of the soccer game. Now I just find this little hole in the ball for me to sink a few teeth into, and I run away with the ball. Jim tries all kinds of tricks to get it back, but I am a bulldog and won't let go. No way. No how. Period.

September 7: So now Jim gives me this floppy Frisbee. He still thinks he can get me to take turns. I just grab the thing and run off with it. I still prefer to play with balls. We do tug-of-war, which is my specialty, but also I can bounce the ball back while jumping up, using my nose.

September 13: Oatley paints not one, but two portraits of me on the walls of our floating home! She can be my godmother whenever and as much as she wants, from now on.

2009

January 24: I get my very own email account. I need help typing. I know what I want to say, and I can get my point across pretty clearly. But my typing is atrocious. Fortunately Mary is really good at typing, and Jim can get by, if he has to.

April 23: I start corresponding with Mary's friend Nessa Forman. She really seems to know some stuff. And I can tell her a thing or two, too. This could be the beginning of a beautiful friendship.

May 21: I am now calling her Auntie Ness, and she takes all kinds of liberties with my name. Just like Jim. I don't mind, as long as the treats keep coming.

July 4: Can you believe it? Again? I don't even want to talk about it.

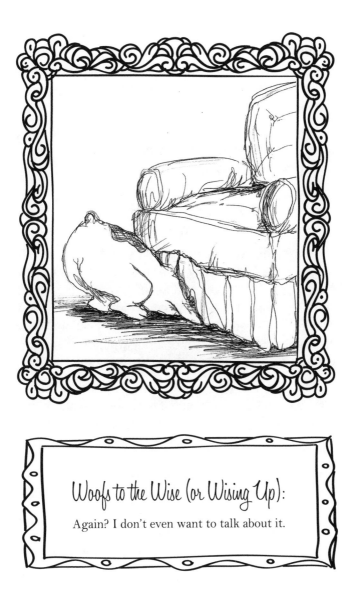

Woofs to the Wise (or Wising Up):

Again? I don't even want to talk about it.

July 15: Auntie Ness comes to visit me! I get to sniff her and give her licks. And she gets to pet me. We take walks together. I wish she could live with us; she understands how important treats are.

July 22: I try to get her to stay, but she had to go home. Back to emails again. She is going to teach me how to be a Diva just like her!

August 11: I fall at the beach while playing tug-of-war and I really hurt my back. We have to go to the doctor's. I think I am okay, but I feel so sleepy now...

September 23: I overhear Mary on the phone with Auntie Ness. Apparently, they're helping me write a book. Well, I wish they had asked me first, but I must confess I think it is a pretty good idea. There are a lot of things that people need to be reminded about. Since clear communicating is another of my specialties, I am just the pooch to do it. So I say, let's go for it!

October and November: Mary, Jim, and I have a few heart-to-heart talks about my book. I think we may have something here. I suggest that Oats do a bunch of drawings of me for the book, so I can pose for her.

2010

January 2: Nobody seemed to want to get much done on this book over the holidays, but now that they are over, we really are starting to move forward. And I am really digging this Diva training.

February 5: This tiny little puppy named Andre just shows up on the dock today. I will have to get him trained fast. Mary says he will grow up to be twice my size, but he needs to know that I'm the big dog around here.

March 23: I chase a beaver from the shore back into the lake to show everyone not to mess with me. Squirrels don't take me seriously; they hang upside down and taunt me. Irritating.

June 18: We are really working hard on this book. I help a lot by adding the really important stuff about Peloton and holiday treats.

July 4: Why does this keep happening? The noise is so bad, I even snap at Peloton when he tries to eat my food, which I normally let him (and only him) do.

August 14: I don't know what happened, but Peloton is gone. Mary tells me he is pretty sick. I hope he gets well quickly, like I did after my back injury. I hope it doesn't have anything to do with my snapping at him.

August 15: Peloton had surgery, but I hear he is okay. But now I am worried because I also hear Mary and Jim talk about Auntie Ness getting sick. What is going on?

August 17: I see Peloton today. We are not allowed to run around, but I give him lots of kisses and I let him kiss me too, which I only let him do on rare occasions. I will visit him every day I can. I wish I could visit Auntie Ness to give her licks and help her get better too.

August 26: Peloton can play again!

October 6: I have a photo shoot at Seattle Pacific University, in my green bra, on their big, well-maintained front lawn. I get to pose any way I like: running, jumping, rolling over, holding a ball, and sitting and standing on guard duty. I wonder what will come of this. A new career, perhaps? I must discuss this with Auntie Ness. I think she must be all better by now.

November 3: I am now a cover girl on the SPU magazine. Well, all right; it's the back cover, but I do get almost a full page. I have the ball in my mouth, looking very protective. The caption says: "Don't drop the ball." As if! Wait until my Auntie Ness hears about this!

November 15: Jim's daughter Joey comes to live in our floating home. We move to stay in the apartment where Mary and I keep our offices.

2011

January 13: It's really cold and gray around here. Too cold for dipping paws into the lake. Too soggy to roll over on the ground.

March 16: Mary is gone. Auntie Ness is really sick now and in the hospital. Mary is staying by her side until she gets better.

June 16: We move back to our cozy home on the lake. We haven't been here for so long; I almost forgot how much fun it is. I get to see Bailey; she still thinks she is the boss of me. I let her have her way a little bit, but I do not concede much anymore. Andre remembers he is not allowed into my house and can only walk by with my permission. This is not negotiable.

July 4: So over it. Moving on.

July 7: Mary has disappeared again. I do not know where she has gone. I think something is seriously wrong again with Auntie Ness. Why can't she get all better, like Peloton? I wish they would explain these things to me. I am always braver when Mary or Jim is around.

July 11: I learn how to listen to Mary on the phone. It's almost as good as having her right here with me, except I don't get the cuddles.

August 5: Jim and I have a new game. He tells me to look away. I agree, because this game is so much fun. Then he says, "Okay." And I get to look for the hidden ball. Over and over. Who knew there were so many places to hide balls?

August 5: I realize that I can hide the ball all by myself! I lift up the corner of one of my day beds and push the ball under. Then I get to find it. I can amuse myself for quite some time doing this.

September 10: This was an awful day. Mary calls Jim. She was with my dear Auntie Ness when she closed her eyes. She won't ever wake up again to come back and see my new tricks. She can't answer my questions any more. I wish she were here so we could take one more walk together. Mary and Auntie Ness were best friends—sorry, sisters-of-choice. And Auntie Ness was the best pen pal and advisor this pooch will ever have.

September 16: Mary is home, and so very sad still. I am too. I keep thinking of things I want to ask my Auntie Ness. I wonder: Could we finish the book without her? Would that play in Peoria? Would she put her money on me?

September 19: I ask Mary for something. I ask her to help me finish our book. I think this could be something big. Maybe it will lead to the big time. I could be a social media superstar. I'll get thousands of "Likes" (and licks) on Facepaw. I'll be a ZZsTreat Blog aggregator. I could be bigger than Lady GaGa. You know what? I think I might be a Diva now.

Woofs to the Wise (or Wising Up):

I wonder: Could we finish the book without her?
Would that play in Peoria?

32

ZZ's Treat: My First-Ever Blog Post

Hello & Woof
Dear Divas-in-Training of the World,

I am ZsaZsa LaPooch. Surely you know who I am. I hear a lot about you from my guardians, Mary and Jim.

I am not just any dog. I am a Diva, and a real original one at that, even though I am only five. I am very cute. I know that because, well, that is who I am. I am a highly evolved Diva at that.

I was trained by the best, my Auntie Ness. I was her apprentice and niecette-of-choice for close to a year. She taught me so many things: how to listen, how to think before I act, and how to use my natural talents in a way that helps everyone in the world. She always said, "Sometimes the family we choose is the best." And she was almost always right about things like that.

I must tell you that I am writing this while feeling a little sad. You see, my Auntie Ness became very ill with cancer. I thought she would get better, because she was so strong. She did not. Just before she died, she told me I was very close to the end of my Diva training and that I would know when my time had arrived. She also told me I had to tell her when it happened.

Auntie Ness, I am a Diva now.

I knew I was a full of Diva-Ness the moment I decided to write this blog. You see, I used to be a therapy dog in Jim's medical practice. My job was to calm people down and make them feel good. I received treats from them, but without realizing it at the time, I gave even more. I gave lots of love and licks. I made people feel good and created good memories for them. That is what my Auntie Ness did for me.

Now I have decided to make it my job to help you achieve the Diva-Ness she knew anyone can achieve. So, to facilitate matters, I am asking you to be my pawpal. I wouldn't mind learning more about you.

Sincerely,

Miss LaPooch

Woofs to the Wise:

Sometimes the family we choose is the best.

Zsa Zsa

About the Authors and Illustrator

Mary M. Mitchell

Mary has written nine books on manners, translated into ten languages, including *The Complete Idiot's Guide to Etiquette* (in its third edition, PenguinPutnam), *The First Five Minutes* (Wiley), *Class Acts* (Rowman & Littlefield), and *Dear Ms. Demeanor* (McGraw Hill). Her newest work is *Fast Track to Manners* (PenguinPutnam).

She has appeared on all the major network morning news and talk shows. Her column, "Ms. Demeanor," which originated in *The Philadelphia Inquirer* (where it ran twice weekly for ten years), was nationally syndicated by King Features. Subsequently, she wrote "Nice Matters" for *The Seattle Times* (two and a half years) and a column on business etiquette for *The Syracuse Post Herald* (two years). She currently writes a column on modern etiquette for Reuters. Mary is frequently quoted in nationally circulated magazines as an etiquette authority.

Through her company, The Mitchell Organization (TheMitchellOrganization.com), Mary has provided training, consulting, and coaching services to major multinational organizations, universities, and nonprofits since 1989. Having lived and worked on four continents, Mary is dedicated to helping individuals become more professional so that they can expand their careers and in turn improve their organizations.

In addition to her writing, coaching, and service to ZsaZsa, Mary is particularly proud to be a certified Zumba® instructor. She is married to Jim Weber and lives in Seattle.

Nessa Forman

Nessa expanded newspaper coverage of the arts in Philadelphia. She served for a number of years as arts and leisure editor for *The Philadelphia Bulletin*. Subsequent to the newspaper's demise, she began a twenty-five-year career with the TV and radio broadcasting station WHYY, retiring as vice president for corporate communications and public affairs in 2007. She was largely responsible for national campaigns promoting "Fresh Air with Terry Gross" on NPR, and "Hometime" and "Liberty's Kids" on PBS.

Following her retirement, Nessa continued to play an influential role in communications and the cultural life of the Greater Philadelphia area. She served as Interim Executive Director of the Gershman Y and consulted for nonprofit organizations, including the Philadelphia Foundation and the Christ Church Preservation Trust.

She also served on boards of numerous cultural and social service agencies, including the Philadelphia Young Playwrights, the library committee of the Philadelphia Museum of Arts, Bread Upon the Waters, and the Caring People Alliance.

Over the years, she worked with colleagues and mentored young professionals to help them tap into their true potential. She was deeply committed to improving the quality of life and educational opportunities for all humans and at least one canine.

Nessa established the Forman Family Fund at The Philadelphia Foundation to provide: education in writing, photography, and architecture for youth; a graduate fellowship in civic history at Temple University; and development of original radio programming at WHYY and organizations meeting basic human needs.

Sadly, Nessa passed away after a valiant struggle with pancreatic cancer in September 2011. She is sorely missed.

Oatley Kidder

Oatley is a well-known muralist in the Los Angeles, Ventura, and Santa Barbara areas. Her pictorial, Chumash Tribal Life, hangs in the Ojai Museum. She has been voted a Lifetime Member of The Ojai Valley Arts Center and currently presides over the visual arts branch of the art center. When Oatley is not on a ladder, you can find her painting in watercolor or pen and ink. Most of her works are commissioned.

An art and animal lover, Oatley is proud to be godmother to ZsaZsa. She and ZsaZsa bonded when she painted murals on the interior of ZsaZsa's houseboat in Seattle, a month-long, in-residence project.

Acknowledgments

From ZsaZsa:

I watch TV with Jim and Mary. Neither would ever admit to watching *Dancing with the Stars* or beauty pageants. But sometimes they leave the TV on while they go off to Dog knows where. So I sit there with one eye open, on the alert for raccoons. And I keep my ears peeled. I hear an awful lot of "Oh my Gods." They also say "Thank God" a lot. Mind you, I think people have that last word backwards, but, just in case they are right and I am wrong, I guess I should thank God too.

I am thankful to my actual parents, Caddis and Bacon, for making me. I cannot remember my mother, but Bacon and I had a sort of play date one time in Dr. Jim's office. He gave me a rather rude correction, and that was that. Why should I associate with any dog, even if he is my father, who lets me have it right in front of the people I work for?

The doctors at Greenlake Animal Hospital get my thanks for performing the operation that brought me and my four sibs to the light of day. John and Kimberly Lorton took it from there and got me off to a healthy start.

Jon and Dana Watling were smart enough to recognize that I was off to an early bossy start and to put the idea in Jim's head of adopting me. Mary was a bit harder to convince, until I won her over by being, as Jon said, "Impossibly cute."

What can I say about how special my guardians are that hasn't been made perfectly clear in my book? I think Jim about summed it up when he said, "If I get to come back, I wouldn't mind coming back as a dog, so long as I have guardians as kind to me as we are to ZsaZsa."

I need to acknowledge that Grisha at Ahimsa inspired me in puppy training school when she called me "ZsaZsa the Brave," even if she never managed to get me to respond to the invitation to "come" unless there is something really special in it for me.

Speaking of treats, I could name all the banks in the Fremont, Ballard, and Eastlake areas of Seattle. Yet one in particular stands out. Union Bank, right across from Epi Apartments, where I have my own office (under the bed), simply stands out ahead of the rest. Not only do they have larger treats, they are happy to see me when I stop in at least once a day. I particularly want to acknowledge Jenn, Sarah, Rosemary, Tai, and Tamara. Dianne left the bank, to my dismay, but left the others with explicit instructions to help me make withdrawals any and every time I come in.

The Epi people have all been great to me. They have been trained to keep on hand plenty of animal crackers for dogs. Amy and Britney always let Jim raid the treat jar. Guy used to be a bit more reticent around me, but I am happy to say that he's coming along; whereas Craig, my special pal, always makes time to scratch me in just the right places.

I want to thank the gardeners who tend to the lawns at the mortuaries and on the Seattle Pacific University campus where I prefer to do my thing.

I am indebted to my godmother Oatley for all the wonderful paintings and drawings.

And I thank my dear Auntie Ness, wherever she has gone, for her patient instructions in the art of Divadom, which I am proud to say I have mastered.

From Mary:

No one ever really writes a book alone. It takes encouragement and support, and frankly, without the encouragement and support of these people, my final promise to Nessa to finish our book never would have been realized.

Jim Weber, ZZ's other guardian and my incomparable husband, is more responsible for this book's completion and its excellence than anyone else, including its authors. He was a tireless contributor, editor, and advocate, keeping me on track when writing through my grief became almost too painful to do. This book is every bit as much his as it is mine, Nessa's, or ZsaZsa's.

It may surprise many of you to learn that Oatley Kidder, our gifted illustrator, never actually met Nessa. Yet, as she listened to me relating the story of this unusual human and canine interaction, she could appreciate its potential visual impact. And this she translated into the series of marvelous drawings that enliven this book. Her efforts embody the treasure that is friendship.

Neil Izenberg gave me a home away from home, compassion, friendship, and home-cooked meals at ridiculous hours each time I made my way back to the East Coast to see Nessa, especially when those visits turned into trips to the ICU and hospice.

Julie Bartha-Vasquez was enthusiastic and helpful in retaining Nessa's voice and spirit. She provided immeasurably valuable editing insights as a former member of Nessa's team at WHYY. Moreover, she has endeared herself to ZsaZsa, Jim, and me.

Caroline Golab, Nessa's other sister-of-choice, never failed to keep the fires of this project burning with her wisdom, wit, and moral support, as well as practical advice. She leads a group of close Nessa pals, all of whom have become the cheerleading squad for this book: Bill Marrazzo, president of WHYY, Sandy Horrocks of Free Library of Philadelphia, Glen Knapp of Philadelphia Young Playwrights, Betsy Anderson of The Philadelphia Foundation, Anne Klein of

Anne Klein Communications Group, Mary Flannery, Randy Plummer, Marlyn Kline, and surely many others I do not personally know.

While I kept my promise to Nessa that our book would be finished, each of you has contributed significantly to ensure that Nessa's inimitable voice—to be read by Sylvia Kauders in the upcoming audio version—will continue to be heard for a long, long time.

Without Kevin Walsh, who introduced me to the extraordinary team at Concierge Marketing, Woofs to the Wise would be floundering in publishing limbo. Instead, Lisa and Ellie Pelto, Sandra Wendel, Erin Pankowski, and Jessica Eckersley turned our project into a book of which Nessa, very much the discerning critic, would have been proud.

Very special thanks go to my cousin Kate Mason. When I told her that I was thinking about getting my first puppy, she instantly replied, "Having a dog will change your life. It will make you a better person." Without her wisdom, I likely would have chickened out.

Thus, ZsaZsa entered Jim's and my life and the lives of Auntie Nessa and many, many others. And she made us all better people, which really is what Woofs to the Wise is all about.

Index

In Memoriam
Nessa Forman

A promise is a promise.

A Note About the Typography

Woofs to the Wise is an etiquette book like no other. Given that it is composed of conversations between a French bulldog, ZsaZsa LaPooch, and a sophisticated Baby Boomer, Nessa Forman, the design team wanted to guide the reader by allowing each voice to be shown through their own distinct font. In addition, Mary M. Mitchell, the author of the book and the narrator of the conversation, also needed a font to set her voice apart. Thus, the text of the book was set in three distinct fonts:

Nessa Forman's voice was set in Arno Pro Regular. Named after the river that runs through Florence, the center of the Italian Renaissance, Arno draws on the warmth and readability of early humanist types of the 15th and 16th centuries. In keeping with Forman's outlook, the font is inspired by the past, but is distinctly contemporary in both appearance and function.

ZsaZsa LaPooch's voice was set in Franklin Gothic, which is modeled on Morris Fuller Benton's original Franklin Gothic, designed in 1902. Named for Benjamin Franklin, Franklin Gothic modernized 19th-century sans serif designs to shape a typeface style that has practically formed a category of its own, just like ZsaZsa LaPooch has done.

Mary M. Mitchell's voice is represented by Arno Italics. Arno Italics was selected as a tribute to Mitchell's place in the world of civility, a distillation of the aesthetic ideals and a refinement of the designer's craft. It is a distinct and readable font, with specific attention to how the letters fit together among each other and as a whole.

The title was set in Filmotype Honey. Originally designed and released in the 1950s, this casual brush script has been remastered to fit today's capabilities. Just like the characters in *Woofs to the Wise*, this font is stylish, energetic, and casual all at the same time.

Zsa Zsa

Foreword Reviews Gives
Woofs to the Wise 5 out of 5 Stars!

What can we learn from a French bulldog about manners? Surprisingly, quite a lot. In a series of email exchanges between Mitchell's French bulldog, ZsaZsa LaPooch, and her long-time friend and "sister-of-choice," Forman, the two strive to share life lessons about manners, civility, and common social interactions. ZsaZsa explains to Forman why she needs to play more, while Forman instructs ZsaZsa on how to be a diva, a subject she prides herself on being an expert in after a lifetime of practice.

In the foreword, Letitia Baldrige, the White House social secretary during the Kennedy Administration, an expert on manners herself, vouches for the soundness of the advice Mitchell and Forman offer. Mitchell has also already established her credibility on the topic as author of *The Complete Idiot's Guide to Etiquette.*

The idea for the unusual correspondence was borne out of a moment of tension that could have potentially led to friction among the friends. Forman, who lived in Philadelphia, was anticipating a visit to see Mitchell and her husband in Seattle. Feeling overwhelmed by

Forman's need to plan every detail of their visit weeks in advance, Mitchell began to communicate with Forman through ZsaZsa, who encouraged her new friend to be more easy-going about the trip, and life in general. She urged Forman to learn to be "in the moment."

The early interactions between ZsaZsa and Forman are amusing and functional. ZsaZsa inquires about Forman's favorite breakfast foods, shampoo, and desired comforts of home, and through their humorous banter, Mitchell learns of her friend's preferences and prepares for her visit. Later email messages cover practical advice about how to be a good hostess and houseguest, and how to deal with the dreaded unannounced guest, as well as more serious subjects, such as how to maintain relationships, why it's important to apologize, and the need to be tolerant of others' faults.

The scenarios discussed are everyday, relatable events, which will appeal to a wide range of ages. The book is geared mostly to women, who often take on the role of organizing social activities among friends and family, but much of the advice can also apply to work settings and to any interactions between people of different age groups.

Kidder's pencil sketches of the characters scattered throughout the book help to establish a playful tone. And when it is revealed that the correspondence had actually served a very important function while one of the women faced a serious illness, earlier exchanges that had initially appeared to be carefree or trivial take on new and profound meaning.

Readers who are willing to go along with the premise of ZsaZsa participating in the discussions will find practical etiquette advice presented in a unique and heart-warming way.

Maria Siano
September 2012

Discussion Questions for Book Clubs

1. How are civility, manners and etiquette different?
2. What are the biggest challenges to civility in today's society?
3. Where do people learn about etiquette today?
4. Should older generations adapt to a less civil society, or should younger generations make a greater effort to learn manners of the past?
5. In the global environment we currently inhabit, is it important to learn cultural differences rather than expecting others to learn yours?
6. Does a successful career depend on good manners?
7. Do men and women have different expectations of what civility means?
8. How important is honesty in the overall view of communication?
9. Can you be a diva and fit nicely into society at the same time?
10. Why is it important for you to differentiate between a personal pet peeve versus a cultural faux pas?

Most Recent Books by Mary M. Mitchell

Are you organizing a group or meeting?

Mary M. Mitchell is adept at speaking to groups of all sizes and generations, whether the focus is career enhancement or a brush up on etiquette. Learn more about Mary at **themitchellorganization.com**, or call today for fees and available dates, 215-284-7975.

Be sure to make **woofstothewise.com**
one of your favorite pages.

Zsa Zsa

My Personal Woofs to the Wise